A Country Girl at Heart

A Country Girl at Heart

by

Peggy Cole

Morrow & Co. Publishers
Bungay . Suffolk
1995

First published, Brechinset Publications 1985
This revised edition, Morrow & Co 1995

ISBN 0 948903 23 6

Designed and typeset by Morrow & Co, Bungay, Suffolk
Printed and bound by the St Edmundsbury Press,
Bury St Edmunds, Suffolk

Contents

Illustrations

Ernie, 1924 - 1980

For
my parents,
husband Ernie,
sons Allan & David,
and brother Ronnie

ACKNOWLEDGEMENTS

There are so many people who have helped me in one way or another to bring this book, both in its original form and this revised edition, into 'flower'.

My sincere thanks to Ronald Blythe for not only writing the Foreword, but also for giving me encouragement, as did the Revd. Cecil and Mrs Adelaide Fox and Norman Scarfe; the staff of Otley College of Agriculture and Horticulture and those of the County Records Office at Ipswich who were always ready to give help and advice; Kim Hartman, Jenny Jones and Janet Charlesworth for their unfailing assistance, and the ladies of the Women's Institute who are always so encouraging.

For constant requests for further books or revised editions, I thank the local bookshops in particular 'The Castle Book Shop' in Framlingham, I say thank you to Karen for her editing and typing of my notes for the revised edition, and to my dear friend Seley for his vetting and invaluable assistance in guidance with the revision.

Finally, I am indebted to Sheila Hardy for her sympathetic editing of the original version.

FOREWORD

I was delighted when Peggy Cole, for so many years a dear friend and neighbour, told me that she was going to write her story because I knew that there was so much in her life, and in her character, which was the very essence of rural East Anglia. The changes experienced by country people since the 1930s have been so extraordinary and far reaching that even those of us who have been caught up in them at the most personal level find it hard to believe that we have lived through such a time. Peggy Cole's story is partly the story of farm-working families up and down the land, and partly an account of how, recently, she emerged via so many truly remarkable activities, and most of all through her wonderful gardening, to become an exponent of country living.

For over a decade now Suffolk has thought of Peggy as its spokeswoman on all kinds of rural matters and I read this calm, truthful statement of 'how it all happened' with admiration. It is open and fresh, and is particularly moving when Peggy writes about her marriage, her sons and parents. A Country Girl at Heart is the achievement of a loved and talented 'village voice', and one which not only I but readers everywhere will welcome.

Ronald Blythe
Bottengom's Farm, Wormingford

INTRODUCTION

It is ten years since I wrote my first book, 'A Country Girl At Heart', many people asked me if I am going to write a sequel. As so much has happened in these ten years, my wish to record these events has guided me towards a revision of the original book.

I was born at Easton in Suffolk, in February 1935. The house where we used to live in Dark Lane is still standing. It was one of those built when the Duke of Hamilton owned the estate. My father was a farm worker, as later was my husband and all my life has been spent in the country. As jobs changed so we moved to different places, but we ended up in Charsfield in my native Suffolk, and there Ernie, my husband and I lived in a Council house with a very large garden, such a large garden in fact, that we were able to cultivate it so that we were able to open it for the public, and as far as I know, we are the only Council house to get a mention in a book of Stately Homes' gardens!

I want to tell you something of my life with my family, the village where we live and some of the wonderful things that have happened in the most unexpected way to me, just an ordinary country girl at heart

Uncle George with his milk 'float'.

THE VILLAGE

Of course the village has changed. How could it stay the same when everything around it has become so different? I don't regret change; everyone feels sad at the passage of the years and the disappearance of things you love, but there is still a village life, and I'm probably right in saying that most of the good things remain, and that is why I want to write about things as they were and how they are now, so if by any chance they do disappear, there is some record in words and pictures of the life and ways that I hold dear.

Sometimes it frightens me to think how quickly the changes have come to our small village. Farming has seen some of the biggest changes, less farm workers needed, fruit-pickers replaced by machines resulting in less work for the women in the fields, and set-a-side making the most noticeable change to the sight of the farmland. I personally do not like to see the fields all overgrown.

We have lost most of the small farms, the ones which grew a small crop and kept a few cattle and chickens, for farming nowadays is big business, and although it has lost much of its quaintness and character, it has also lost a good deal of its hardship and oppressiveness. We still have The Hall, Red House Farm and Prospect Farm whose owners' family name has been going just on a hundred years, but the small ones with names that showed their location like Valley, Brook and Well and the others called after the trees amongst which they were set have disappeared as the land has been sold off to make bigger and more economic units.

Nobody comes round to the village anymore to sell groceries, bread and meat etc. Thank goodness we still have our daily newspaper delivered, milk however only arrives every other day. We do have a bus service six days a week, but for how

5

long? That is the question. The village Primary School is still going strong, with 40 plus children, and we still have the 'Local' pub. Numbers are diminishing at the local church, and the chapel has no permanent Minister.

When I was a girl you got your milk and butter from Shrubbery or Buttons Farms. Shrubbery Farm did a proper milk round. Ernie's stepbrother, George Mead, now eighty years, retired several years ago as stockman at the farm, started the milk round by carrying a couple of churns in a box on the front of a trade cycle, using 1/2 pint and 1 pint measures to dole out the customer's requirements at the door. He later progressed to a motor-cycle with a side-car and finally to a small van. Buttons Farm sold milk and butter at the door. The farmer then, the late Mr. G. Goudy, always used to sow swedes with his cattle beet, so in the winter months when his customers bought their milk and butter they could also buy a swede, often as big as you could carry, for a halfpenny. These are very tasty when cooked, especially if mashed with a good lump of butter. This farm also sold off the skim that was left after the butter was made. This was usually fed to calves, but it might be sold off cheaply to poor families. It's a funny old world, isn't it? whoever would have thought the day would come when it would be fashionable for the diet conscious to drink skimmed milk, or that it would cost the same, if not more than full cream milk.

Mr Goudy, by the way, was the last old gentleman that I can remember in the village to wear breeches and buskins, those pieces of stiffened leather with buttons all down the side which wrapped around the legs from ankle to knee. Ernie used to say that Friday was the best day to call round at Buttons Farm as the smell of Mrs Goudy baking bread in her old brick oven and brewing beer in the old copper was wonderful.

Most householders made their own bread in those days if they could, but if they didn't have a brick oven then they either had to walk into Wickham Market to buy their loaves or rely on Mr Baldwin the baker from Woodbridge who started his deliveries in the 1920s with a horse and cart and then progressed to a van. If you did make your own bread, then you probably bought your bundles of faggots to burn in the oven from the two brothers who called. They charged 3/- for 20 bundles, and I am told they wouldn't deliver less than a score at a time.

It seems hard now to believe that the village once had six shops, a post office and three boot repairers. I can't remember two of these, but I do remember taking our shoes to the late Mrs Keeble who carried on the business when her husband died. She had a little shed in the backyard. There were three butchers, two being part of other shops, and most of the shops sold pork in some form, like the late Mrs Alice Johnson who was famous for her pork cheeses and Millie Males who was well known for her pork scraps. Then there was Mr Brickie Harvey who would go in his horse and cart to get fresh fish from Aldeburgh which he would smoke in an old tin shed and then later take round the village to sell.

Every village must have two or three men who can turn their hand to most things, including cutting their mates hair. At one time we had two gentlemen who would perform this service if you went to their homes, while the late Mr Harsnet, who ran the cycle repair shop, was always ready to oblige with a haircut, but in 1947 George started his own little business. He bought an old bus off his boss, the late Mr L.W. Pudney, which had been used for a meal shed, painted it green and had it stand on the side of the road in Chapel Lane. For many years he did good service, then the rates people came along and George was forced to put up his prices to cover the cost of the rates. He used to charge 6d. for men and 3d. for children. Our sons Allan and David used to love going to see Uncle George for their haircuts every four weeks and there would be a rush to see who could get into the bus first to read the comics, of which George always had a plentiful supply. They never minded how long they had to wait for their turn, which was just as well as it was used very much as a meeting place, especially by the pensioners who were quite happy to sit and discuss the latest news in the village. The business operated

7

Uncle George's barber's hut

every Tuesday and Thursday from 6 p.m . till 8.30 p.m. In the winter months George cut hair by the light of the oil lamps which hung from the roof and the place was kept warm and cosy by the oil stove that stood in one corner. It was a sad day for a great many old village boys when George packed up the business in 1965.

The old bus ended up beside Charsfield United football ground near the local river where it stood on four cast iron wheels, but eventually it got so rotten it had to be burnt down. But George still goes round to cut the hair of any old boy who is housebound.

Another job George carried out for over forty years is chimney sweeping. I have seen him go many a mile round the villages on cycle with his sweep's brushes balanced on his back. And last, but by no means least, he wound up our church clock for more than twenty-five years.

And talking of cycling, there was a woman in the village who for over forty-four years, cycled in all weathers, never missing a day to fetch and deliver from Woodbridge to us and other villages along the way our daily newspapers. A dear kind soul, who was sorely missed when she retired.

We don't have a blacksmith anymore, though once there were two just for shoeing horses. But then nowadays, there isn't a farm in the village keeping a working horse, though several people keep some for riding. The local undertaker has gone too, as has the local grave digger. There is no longer any need for the hurdle maker to provide the 50 or 60 hurdles a shepherd required to make up a pen or sheepfold; nowadays electric fencing does the same job.

Neither do we have a regular carrier service. There are those who can still remember the time when the carrier used a horse and cart which in the 1920s was replaced by Mr J. Grout's van. Then came Mr Copping who ran a bus and carrier service. George's late wife Hilda remembered riding in Copping's charabanc for the Sunday School treat to see the sea at Felixstowe.

Then Mr Soames from Otley started his service. This used to

9

come round the villages twice a week doing four trips to Ipswich. Many a time I have been on the bus and seen the driver stop at a house or farm where there was a notice on the hedge which read 'Soames'. Down would get the driver and off he would go to the door of house or farm to ask what it was he was to pick up in town. It could be some shopping, or an extra large parcel, or perhaps a bottle of medicine, or some animal feed, or maybe it was a recharged accumulator needed to run the old wirelesses we had in those days. Nothing was too much trouble for these drivers. I am always very grateful for their kindness towards my dad. He used to go on the bus regularly to watch Ipswich Town play in the 1950s, and when in later years he got more and more shaky with his Parkinson's Disease, one of Soames's drivers would look out for him, even keeping the bus waiting till he got there if he was a bit late after the match was over.

Which reminds me of the tale of the old gypsy, known as Fiddler Bill, not, I might add, because he played that instrument! Well, he used to walk to Ipswich each week, but one day, the driver of the bus stopped and asked if he wanted a lift. Bill thanked him kindly, but refused the offer, adding "I'm sorry, but I'm in a hurry!"

That's another sign of the times. We no longer have gypsy families living in the village. The last one I remember was in the 1950's. She lived in a cottage and used to walk miles round the surrounding villages pushing an old pram which had the pickles, cottons, silks and other bits and pieces she had for sale. And nowadays we don't get the tramps either who used to call at the back door for a cup of hot water or a crust of bread. Ernie could recall the days when the tramps would pass through the village during the morning after they had been turned out of the Workhouse at Wickham Market where they had spent the night.

Another traveller, now long gone, was Mr 'Stumpy' Fisk. He had a donkey (or dickey, as we say in Suffolk) to pull his cart in which he collected not only old rags and bones, but also rabbit skins at a penny a time and moleskins too, though he expected these to have been pegged out on a board and dried before he would buy them. You have to remember that in the old days a few extra coppers meant an extra bit of food on the table, and most families had two maybe three rabbits a week to eat. I still like rabbit when I can get one but after I have skinned mine the skin goes on the compost heap.

For a long time Mr Chapman was another who cycled many miles with a cart behind his bicycle bearing the tools of his trade, but it is many a year since we have had anyone else to clean our windows. Even the coal was delivered by cart in the 1920s when Mr E. Taylor had his business. George can remember the time when all the best oak trees in a nearby wood called Old Park were cut down by the Stowmarket Timber Company. It would have been just after the First World War, and all the wood chips, those bits which were cut out to get the tree down, because of course, they were all hand cut then, were sold off at 3d. a tree. George and his mother used to push the pram two miles to this wood and fill it up. It was reckoned that one pram full would just about hold threepence worth of firewood.

Times were very hard then and often the farm labourer and his family had to fall back on two other seasonal jobs to help make a few extra pence. One was Stone Picking. The stones were taken up from the fields and used to help keep the roads in reasonable repair in the days before they were properly surfaced. Each picker, and often these were women and children, would have a two-gallon bucket which held about a peck of stones. When the bucket was full it was emptied into a heap which had to be made into a load of about 70 bucketsful. For this you might receive the grand sum of 3/- (about 15p). My auntie did this job when she was young, wearing an apron made from an old sack in which to carry the stones. It was, without any doubt, very hard work, but often it was the difference between being able to have the money to buy a pair of boots for a child and not.

Much less hard and boring was Brushing. This took place in the pheasant and partridge shooting season. The local men and young boys were hired by the owners of the big estates to go beating through the undergrowth to set the game birds flying. When Ernie first started, they worked from about nine in the morning until about four, or as long as the light lasted, and when they had finished shooting then the gentlemen 'passed the hat round' and the money was shared amongst the men. There was also a free pint of beer. Nowadays, the men earn a standard fee for the job, and get two cans of beer. Thirteen is the usual number of brushers on a shoot, which are still held regularly in our locality, but quite often girls and women take part, and often the parties are tourists from France, who have come on a package deal which includes dinner at the farmer's house after the shoot.

That's one side of life that has changed. So too have the visits of the doctors. In the 1920s the doctor used to come from a village four miles away by horse and cart, and I have been told by one old chap in the village that when the doctor was called to attend a birth, you were expected to have the gin bottle ready for him to have his drink before he started work. He also told of the vet at the same time who always called at the pub first before coming to see a sick animal, often arriving at the farm almost unable to stand up.

Fortunately things like that no longer occur, they are like the visits of the knife-grinder and the oil-man who bought the oil for the lamps which lit our homes, now just fading memories.

As are some of the events and pastimes of my girlhood and the youth of my parents. In those days there were few 'events' to brighten up the brief time off we had, but I suppose that made them seem that more important. Woodbridge Horse Show, the Ipswich Horse Parades and the Framlingham Gala were the main entertainments in the early 1900s. Woodbridge held its Horse Show on Easter Monday, the Gala at Framlingham was on Whit Monday. Most people in our villages thought nothing of walking the ten or twelve miles each way to attend these events.

At the Horse Parades, any of the animals which had not been subjected to the four 'P's' - Paint, Polish, Perseverance and

Pride - did not stand and earthly chance of carrying off anything except a judges reject. Ipswich Corporation dispensed with their last two horses in March 1951. It is a shame that the working horse has all but disappeared. Ernie and my brother Ron used to work with horses with names like 'Prince', 'Boxer' and 'Valley Duke'. They got pleasure from working with another living being that could, in its own way, communicate with them, unlike a machine. Ernie was a horseman for seven years before we married. He always reckoned that we might see more use made of the horse in the future as fuel becomes more expensive for both machines and fertilisers.

A Furrow Drawing or a Ploughing Match was very popular in the days before the tractor came. My grandfather used to enter these competitions, where the first prize was a copper kettle for ploughing the straightest furrow, sometimes called 'the best stretch'. To qualify, the furrow had to have a good finish with the neatest and most level top. One ploughman would walk miles to watch others at work, no doubt weighing up the competition, and woe betide the poor chap whose ploughing was not in line, he was likely to be the topic of conversation at the pub for several nights. Sometimes a winner of a ploughing match would take the prize money of 12/6 instead of the kettle, as this was more than a week's wages, but usually, there was great pride in owning a kettle which was then handed down as a family heirloom, although I know that eventually many kettles ended up in the hands of antique dealers as a result of hard times.

When we had to make our own entertainment, things were a lot livelier. Now to a large extent, that 'magic box', the television, has taken much of the zest out of village recreation, although over the years, the Mothers' Union, the Forget-Me-Not-Club for the over sixties, the Womens' Institute, the Boys' and Girls' Brigades, with their meetings, football teams, talks and quizzes as well as the organised events of the Church and Chapel still give us a lot to do, but I want to tell you about some of the village games we played as children and the ones

13

that are still played in the village pubs.

TIP IT was played by men in the pub. The contestants sit on forms on both sides of a table and a small object, known as 'the piece' is passed from hand to hand. All hands are clenched and then placed on the table and one of the opposing team tips the hand he thinks holds the piece. This is repeated three times and then it is the turn of the other side. Of course stakes are decided before the game starts. I suppose this is almost a silent form of 'Call My Bluff'.

QUOITS was very popular at one time. There are, I believe many versions of the game, but the one that I was told was played behind the pub and involved a circular board about 13" in diameter and painted white except for a narrow black line around the edge. There is another circle in the centre of the board about 4" diameter and a black dot right in the middle. The board is also marked off into quarters and numbered. The quoits were made of rubber, approximately 2 1/2" in diameter and each player had three. The object of the game was to score as close to 18 as possible by clearing the lines in the different sections, the centre giving the highest score of course.

My bit of Suffolk has a great tradition of marble playing and when I was a child we used to play some of these variations during the spring. For *LONG TAW* each player placed a marble in a row about four feet apart. A mark was then made about six feet from the first marble and the first player took up his or her position on the mark and attempted to hit the first marble. If it was hit, it was won and another attempt was made at the next and so on until all the marbles had been won. If the player failed to make a hit, the next player took over.

LITTLE RING involved each player putting a marble into a ring on the road about 18" in diameter. Then the players each rolled a shooter marble from a given distance towards the ring, the object being to knock the others out of the ring. If there was plenty of space available one could extend the circle to four or five feet across, in which case you were then playing *BIG RING*. *TRACING* was a progressive sort of game that we played on the way to school, the object being to bypass each other while trying to hit and win your opponents marble. For some reason, *DIBBLE HOLE* was played only by girls. A hole was made in the ground with the heel of your shoe, and from an arranged distance each player would roll a marble towards the hole. The one who was nearest to the hole would try to get it right in by flicking it with the index finger. If she did so, she went on to the next one, but if she failed the next player had a turn and so on until all the marbles had been won.

Every marble player had a special marble which he used for most games. There was the Ring Toy which was a large granite marble about the size of a table tennis ball. With one of these a player stood a good chance of knocking several marbles out of the circle in one go. There was also a Glass Alley about the same size as the granite one which we called Domshees. If your Domshee stopped in the ring it had to stay there until it was knocked out, and during that time you were out of the game. The most popular marbles were the Ginger Pop marbles obtained from the neck of a lemonade bottle, the Blood Alley which was made of pottery and had a thin red vein in it, and the Crag which was a trifle larger with blue and green lines quartering it.

Both boys and girls enjoyed bowling hoops. The boys had iron ones which they bowled with an iron hook, the girls were more likely to have wooden ones, but just as much fun could be had using the old rim of a bicycle wheel or a perambulator wheel. Boys also went in for pea shooters made from elder wood and pop-guns which, using compressed air, could fire acorns a fair old distance. The wire spring taken from a lady's corset was also turned into a weapon of sorts.

We also played Hopscotch, that is the girls did, during the summer, using a spiral figure rather than the set of squares that is sometimes seen. And of course at Easter time we played whip and top, then it was the turn of the skipping rope to come into fashion and in the autumn we had the inevitable conker fights. Some of these games still survive, but sadly, there are fewer and fewer children in the village to play them.

For the grown-ups The Three Horseshoes was the place for a

Saturday night out. Here the farming folk would meet to talk over the news of the week, discuss their different progress on the farm, have a drink, play cards or one of the other pub games, or even have a dance and a sing-song.

We sang songs to the accompaniment of one or more accordions or mouth organs. We had our own type of dancing which was known as 'Step Dancing', quite exciting in its way as there was no particularly fixed pattern of stepping and no two dances were identical. It was often the local gypsies who were the best at this with their rollicking and wild music. Sometimes I'm afraid that the excitement and the beer got too much and it often ended up with a bit of fighting, but never the vicious stuff that you hear about nowadays. Mind you, I don't know how people afforded to get drunk in those days because in the days of my youth, although beer was 4d a pint, agricultural wages were around thirty shillings a week on which to feed and clothe a family of five or six. I imagine that the menfolk took up fighting so they could stretch the time out longer in between pints. Besides which, getting knocked out is a good way of making sure that you don't have to buy the next round.

In my mind the best thing about a night out at the pub was the singing, because it was when a man or woman stood up to sing, without any ceremony save that of the good feelings of those around, that you saw, in a strange sort of way, the light and the humanity shine out of him. In a way I suppose, it was like a rustic church without the religion, although in many ways, you could say that the religion was there wrapped up in life.

We have been talking about events of different kinds and I suppose the two main events in any one's life are birth and death, although strangely enough these are the events you don't personally remember! That's why, I suppose, the Church remembers them for us. And in between life and death the Church tends to be the central point in the village for other events. If you want to know my favourite church, then of course it is St. Peter's, Charsfield, the lovely old twelfth-century building where I was married, and where I have the families close to me married, and where I have witnessed the christenings and the funerals of some of my loved ones. Here too have been the ordinary Sunday services and the special ones and in this old church I have spent many, many happy hours giving my own form of praise to God by helping to decorate with flowers to celebrate the different festivals like Easter, Christmas and Harvest Thanksgiving.

Hoo Church is my second favourite, and has now become my regular place of worship, the reason being that they still hold the 'Old Church Prayer Book' services, and also the 8.30 a.m. service now suits me due to my hectic weekends with visitors to my garden. When I go to Hoo Church I feel close to my father and his generation. Perhaps it's because they all worked on the farm next to the churchyard. We did the funeral scene for the film Akenfield in Hoo Church, but I'll tell you about that later on. Mentioned in the Domesday Book, Hoo has one of the oldest churches in one of the smallest villages. Unfortunately, like many more it needs thousands of pounds to remain an active Church. I hope that when you come down this way, as well as visiting me, you will go and have a look at both these churches. You see, I don't like mere talk about things, sometimes I don't understand what religious people are talking about when they give these learned sermons. To me religion is really life. Everybody's living, and so everybody is together. We all come together in the Church and I think it is interesting to see how it encompasses our lives.

Each day I see signs of birth around me as the cycle of life is always turning in my garden. After the hardness of some winters the fact that so many flowers have sprung into new life and bloomed again, makes me believe that there must be a Creator. But nowadays, how many women think of going to church to thank God after childbirth? A few years ago it would have been unheard of, certainly in a village, for a woman to go out anywhere before she had been 'churched'.

And in a similar way the ritual of death is also disappearing. I believe that you have to mourn when you lose a loved one, it is

17

part of the healing. It is good to talk about those who have died and to remember their love and care, these are bitter sweet experiences. But there are those who try to shut out what has happened, who carry on as if nothing has changed. But if you can't honour death, then what price for human dignity in the short space you are alive? Perhaps in the country it's easier to come to terms with death because you are much more aware of the eternal cycle of life and death. There was in the village a certain farm worker, who having paid for some time an insurance policy towards the cost of his funeral made up his mind he would pay no longer. The insurance agent tried long and hard to persuade him against such a step. At last the old boy said "Look you here, bor, I isn't going to pay no more, 'cos if my friends don't bury me for love, then they will for stink!"

HOUSING

You might be interested in the population figures for Charsfield this century, for they help to show the changes in the countryside.

Year	Population
1921	369
1931	416
1961	298
1978	370
1984	380
1992	390

The population just sort of increased naturally until the late thirties, but then there was a big drop in the figures during the Second World and the years after. Five of the men from the village were killed on active service, including Ernie's brother Russell, but the main reason for the decline was that the introduction of new machinery and technology in farming meant that fewer men were needed to work on the land, so there was a drift away from the village to find new jobs in the town. You may wonder why there was such an increase in the seventies. Well that's the new estate for professional people and others who work in town but like the idea of living in the country. I don't complain about this 'invasion' because most of the people are quite keen to become involved in village life, although there are a few who never do.

The housing situation has not increased since the new estate, there are no new ones, and if the village doesn't look as if it has changed much on the outside, I can tell you that most of the houses have changed on the inside, and for the better. I'd say. I mean you don't get many things like the 'Old Bumby' any more. The photograph on page 23 is of my grandad's outside closet, the only part left when the cottages were modernised. I suppose it was a wonderful invention if you wanted to get outside on a nice day and have a think, but you can take it from me that in the cold and dark, the Old Bumby was not the most exciting of prospects. We still have one left in the village even today. (1995)

The first barn conversion has taken place in the village, how many more will follow! I wonder. Mind you it is good that the old buildings are put to use in this way.

At the turn of the century, most of the houses were made of stud and plaster, that is a timber framework covered with plaster, clap board or weather boarding or brick. There were no built-in bathrooms, and the privy was not only as close to nature as you could get, but also shared with your neighbours. The cottages were mostly of the two up, two down variety with an added scullery or 'back-us'. (In those houses where a staff was kept, the odd-job boy was often called the 'Back-us' boy. Ernie was known as this when he started his first job in the farm house.) Windows were usually small and the floors made of red brick were so uneven that we had to have wedges under one or more of the legs of pieces of furniture to keep them level. These brick floors were lovely breeding grounds for the cockroaches who made their nests in the bindweed which grew up between the bricks. We used coconut matting to cover the floor and in front of the hearth was a large black and red mat made out of bits of old cloth by my mother. There was also an old thick sack by the door to keep out the draught.

An oak beam ran through the cottage and over the fireplace was the lintel beam. Also above the fire was the mantel-shelf from which hung a pretty border of red velvet or chenille which was fringed with little bobbles. These of course went out when the modern tiled and stone fireplaces came in, but I've still got a beautiful one given me by my late Aunt Liz which she used in the 1920s.

Walls in these old cottages were papered, not once, but many times. The paper was much thicker then anyway, and to help keep the draughts out and to straighten a saggy wall, you never took off a paper when it was time to decorate, you just stuck the next lot on top. Sometimes, the underneath layers dried out and left gaps, and then it was possible at night to hear the crickets which lived between the layers.

Talking of draughts, I can remember as a small child seeing mum push balls of newspapers into those large old keyholes we had to keep out the howling wind, as well as pushing papers and rags under and around the front door for the same reason. No wonder the front door was only ever opened for weddings and funerals.

The staircase, rotten with worm holes, was so narrow that sometimes you had to go up it on all fours. Of the two bedrooms the biggest would be for the parents, but there might be a bit of room curtained off for the child or children who slept in the parents' room. The other room would just about hold a double bed for the rest of the children. In some families, the boys and girls slept top and bottom.

The chimney-breast usually took up a lot of room in the bedrooms so the only furniture was likely to be a chest of drawers, and perhaps a chair if you were lucky, but most likely, you hung your clothes on the bedroll when you took them off at night, or, in winter months laid them on top of the covers to keep you warm. It has been known for father's overcoat to go over the top of all!

In the middle of the living room stood the large table with its well scrubbed white deal top and the plain wooden chairs around it. Under the window was a chest of drawers, the family Bible and the lamp on the top of it. The brass paraffin oil lamp was precious and had to be looked after very carefully. I used to watch mum take the long funnel glass of and with a stick wound round with a soft cloth she would gently clean the inside being very careful not to poke the stick through the side of the glass, which could snap very easily. Then you had to turn the wick up and cut it level, and God help you if you

21

didn't get that wick straight for it would smoke you to hell, blacken the glass all down one side and you would have to start the whole thing again.

The fireplace was often a large black open grate, polished with Zebra grate polish until you could see your face in it. If the hearth was white, then this would be cleaned with hearthstone, a white block dipped in water and wiped with a rag.

There was nothing much about the kitchen to write home about - or anywhere else for that matter, as it was often a dark and dank old place. Just a wooden bench to hold the bowls for washing and the pails of water, because of course there was no water laid on in these cottages. An enamelled jug stood on a tin plate to catch the drips, used for filling the smoke-blackened kettle. A few shelves on the walls held the small quantity of cooking pots and saucepans. On the back door was the roller towel. Up to mum's last years she had her roller towel rack which we moved from house to house, always fixing it to the back door.

Also kept out here and helping to add to the various smells of the kitchen were the candles which we used, especially for going up to bed. I can still see, in my mind's eye, the everyday tin plate candle holders, their trays full of the rehardened tallow which had dripped as the candle burned unevenly, perhaps because of a draught. And the eerie shadows these candles cast.

In the autumn, my father used to store apples for our later use under our beds, and many's the time my sisters and I have thought that we would pinch one to eat in bed, but when we put the candle down to see what we could get, the shadows that reflected back at us mixed with our guilty consciences were enough to send us back snuggling under the blankets.

The copper in which we used to boil our washing was usually in the kitchen, though occasionally it stood in the corner of the scullery. The cast iron container which held about

Grandad's 'Old Bumby" - the outside closet!

ten gallons of water was housed in a brick structure about 3' x 3'. Beneath the copper was an open fire but there was a little cast iron door which held the burning fuel in. You could burn almost anything under the old copper, wood paper, even old rags. If possible we used rain water as this is nice and soft, if not we would put in a handful of soda. The old block soap was eventually replaced with Persil, but to start the wash, several bowlsful of water were drawn from the copper and put in the big wash tub and all the linen was washed by hand, then the white linen was put into the copper itself and given a good ten minute boil, stirred occasionally with a two feet long 'copper stick' which over the years became as white as the linen itself. How many children I wonder, lived in fear of having the copper stick laid across their backside?

The dirty water from the washing was taken out and emptied into a big hole at the bottom of the garden, and the copper refilled to give us hot water for the rest of the day, our luxury for the week until the bath was required at the weekend. When we rinsed the washing, all the whites went into water that had had a 'blue-bag' dabbled in it, the pale blue water somehow gave that extra white look. Finally, there was the business of putting the washing through the mangle to squeeze out all the excess water before hanging the linen on the line. We had a great contraption which stood about four feet high and had two large rollers made of wood and a cast iron handle to turn them. One day, when I was small, I was so annoyed with brother Ron that I pushed his fingers through the rollers. I am ashamed to say that I badly bruised his hand.

Of course, after all the washing comes the ironing, and in those days it was done with a flat iron heated on top of the cooking stove or the oil stove. Mum used to heat hers on the trivet, that little platform on front or to the side of the fire grate on which we could stand the kettle or a saucepan. When the iron became hot, you rubbed it first on a piece of coarse cloth or sacking to make sure it was clean.

Cooking was done in my young days on an oil stove. There was the type with a single burner on which you could boil a kettle or a saucepan, and then there was the sort which had two or three burners and a metal frame on which a box type oven was put. To use an oil cooking stove you need to be a good judge, because there is no temperature control on them, and the higher the wick was turned up, the larger and more fierce were the flames, so you had to watch carefully. Nowadays with a modern oven, a few buns will cook in twenty minutes, but with the oil stove it might be an hour or more, so you certainly needed that celluloid window in the front of the stove to let you see how the food was cooking. Mind you, the old stove has its uses. It's particularly good for slow cooking, and I still use mine when I have a pig's head to cook for making brawn.

When you look back those old houses were steamy and draughty, with the smells of cooking, washing, living and sleeping all mixed up with the oil and paraffin smell of the lamps and the wood smoke of the fire. I suppose they were more like nests than houses. The ones that came after them seem to have struck a happy medium. Mine, as you will hear later, is a Council house, built before the war and I think it is warm and cosy as well as being as comfortable as you can ask for. Very different from some of these new houses that are all glass and wood. There is the new estate with its 'executive' houses and two others have got this solar heating. All these houses have four or even six bedrooms and two lavatories and are now quite normal. My sons now live in a centrally heated house with a kitchen full of automated electrical machines, washer, fridge and freezer, and when they married, they bought all their furniture in one go, not like us for whom it took a lifetime, piece by piece, room by room. Now, I can't make judgements as to the quality of life and how it has changed. Obviously, it is a lot easier for a lot of people. For a start, we most of us live longer and have more holidays, and more than that, here am I writing a book, when years ago I would have neither the time nor yet encouragement for such a thing. But there again, just take a loaf of bread that you make yourself. If you have to prepare the oven, get the ingredients right and use your skill to make it; if you see it through all its

25

various stages, and can smell it while it's cooking, then by golly, it doesn't half taste that much better when you come to eat it.

Mum giving a hand with the turkey plucking, December 1974

MY FAMILY

My mother came from Waldringfield, a little village just the other side of Woodbridge, well known for sailing as the river Deben runs on the edge of the village. Her father worked on the land, and when she was old enough mother went into service as a parlour-maid to the doctor in Melton. She lived in and had a half day off a week and one Sunday in three. She had a cycle fitted with old carbide lamps and many times she has told me of how frightened she was as she cycled back to work after visiting her parents along dark roads and lanes made even more dark by very high hedges. I never knew my grandmother for she died at the age of fifty when I was two. Mother had just one sister.

Dad, on the other hand, had two brothers and six sisters. He too came from a farm labourer's family in Kettleburgh. He went into the Regular Army in 1919, serving in the Suffolk Regiment in Gibraltar and in India, and as I look through his service record book, it says that dad was smart, intelligent, clean, sober, reliable and trustworthy. Dad was a good scholar, not only could he add up very quickly, but he could spell anything you asked him, though when we were small and asked him to spell a word for us, he would always say first, "Don't you larn anything at school?"

When dad came out of the Army in 1926 with medals from the Indian Rebellion, he went on to the land, working with his father at Hoo Hall. I don't know how soon it was before he met mother, but I do know from my late Aunt Liz that dad used to cycle to Melton most nights to see mum. This was a trip of about eight miles and often he would be late home. She said he would try to creep in without the rest of the household hearing him, but unfortunately there were a couple of stairs that creaked and groaned and even though he tried to miss them out, they would somehow still give him away, and when his father called him for work - at 4.30 a.m. because he was a cowman, grandfather would say, "Come on, you ain't been there long. I heard you come in." Mum and dad married in 1934 and went to live in a little cottage in Easton.

My father was a general farm worker cum stockman, working in the fields most of the day and feeding the animals morning and night, every day of the week including weekends. He wages were like those of all other agricultural workers at that time very poor, about 30/- and it was essential to earn that extra 5/- for the weekend's work. Holidays were unheard of and we never went away for one with our parents, and I can't even remember dad going with us to the seaside for the day when we all went on the Sunday School outing. Dad's spare time was taken up with two part-time gardening jobs, and he also did a lot of hedge cutting to get wood for the winter. One year a friend of dad's had a circular saw which was run off a belt from the tractor. You had to hold the long pieces of wood on the saw bench for the saw to cut into small pieces. On this particular weekend, Ron and I stood watching the wood being cut when all of a sudden dad cried out and we saw him shake his arm. He had caught his hand on the saw and split open his thumb and finger. He was taken to hospital and had to stay in for a long time. Mum has since told me what a worry this was for them as there was not much money coming in, not like the sickness benefits of today, and she was so short that she didn't know where to find the shilling for the insurance man when he called.

At weekends dad would take us to the farm with him and we would try to help in our little way with the feeding of the animals. We would, for instance, turn the handle of the large cutter which chopped the cattle beet into three inch strips. Then we mixed chaff and meal with Kositos turning the heaps over and over. We loved Kositos, it was like corn flakes and when no one was looking we'd pick bits out to eat. The smell of the mixture was lovely.

The next job was to help dad shovel it all up into pulp bags

Sugar Beeting - 1933
Dad on the extreme right, grandfather third from left

and it was then ready for when the animals needed feeding. Sometimes we were allowed to help feed and put hay in the boxes of the Suffolk horses. There was one, Boxer, a huge beast with great big, greasy legs that we were scared to go near in case he kicked, but even so, one of our biggest treats came when we went to meet dad bringing the horses home for tea and he would stop and put us on their backs for the last ride home. Mind you, it was pretty frightening when the horses made straight for the pond in the farmyard for a long drink and they stretched their necks down into the water. Dad would shout, "Hold tight! You'll be all right." We hung on to those manes like grim death!

At harvest time we took dad his tea in the fields, mum would pack us a little bag with bread and jam and a bottle of lemonade to have with him. We lived on bread and jam in those days. Dad used to have Oxo and bread when he got up for work and then bread and cheese for his bait time (the meal taken at work). We used to have bread, marg and brown sugar for our breakfast, never butter. Dinners were mainly stews and suet puddings. Dad used to call his food "whittles" as did most of the other farm workers in my young days. You would hear them in the harvest field when they were cutting corn say, "Here come the missus with the whittles". In the afternoons you might hear them talking about Beevers or Fourses for their four o'clock tea-break. My late husband still used 'Fourses' for his cup of tea at the weekend. And I still make Suffolk rusks and stickies, bits of left over pastry rolled out with a few currants and a little sugar and baked flat, just like mum did.

Dad made us a little cart out of an orange box and two pram wheels, and when we got old enough we would go sticking at the weekend. We would bring bits of wood home for the copper fire and fir cones to help out with the kindling. We also used to pick rose hips and blackberries and these mum would sell in Framlingham. We also got one penny a pound for acorns from the local farmer. He used them to help feed his pigs.

Dad's pride and joy was his garden so woe betide us if a ball

30

ever went on it, it would be a quick clip on the ear if he found out. Like grandad he produced some lovely vegetables and flowers, and often people would pull up at the gate to see if he had any for sale. One year he sold some flowers to a Nursery called Toogood Bros. The receipt reads like this:-

1/2 oz. Candytuft   -9d.

1/2 oz. Larkspur   -1s.9d.

6 lbs. Sweet Pea seeds -£9.12s.0d.

Mum told me you would have thought that dad had won the football pools when he received this money. They bought a new secondhand three-piece suite with some of the money. She said dad was very good about money, he often gave her extra if he had done more overtime or if his gardening jobs brought him more than he expected.

On a Saturday and Sunday evening in the summer we would walk from Easton to Kettleburgh to see grandad, and then the two men would go into the smoke room of "The Chequers" for a drink while mum and I sat outside with the pram with Ron in it. I remember my grandfather as a very stern man with white hair, smoking a clay pipe. When we visited him dad always warned us not to walk over the plants in his garden or to go near his bees. But he was kind to his children and whenever one visited there was always a supply of fruit and vegetables to take away with them if they wanted it. Grandad's vegetables were reckoned to be the best for miles around. He had lots of secrets about how he achieved such results, but he wouldn't part with them. But we all knew that he emptied his bumby into a long trench across the garden and then planted his celery on top.

Grandad of course was a keen competitor at all the local shows. Aunt Lizzie told of how when she was a child they were all put to bed early the night before a show, so that

31

grandad and grandmother could get the soft fruit ready on plates for the following morning. He used to show red, white and black currants nearly as big as cherries. The children would wait until the parents were in the garden and then slip down to pinch a string of fruit. After they had been caught doing this, grandad decided to take all his precious entries across the road to the old Water Mill where great-grandfather lived. Aunt Lizzie said they were not allowed to touch the fruit on the bushes, but they thought they ought to make sure that they had a taste. She said they were all set out on plates covered with leaves, the fruit all on strings, looking fit for a king.

He also used to show his honey, mead made from it, and beeswax, poured into egg cups and tumblers to make it into interesting shapes. Nowadays it is only at the very big shows that you see beeswax on display. Grandmother also entered the shows, and won first prize for many years with her brown and white breads. Aunt Lizzie also remembered that on show days all the children had to have their Saturday wash very early, then put on their best white pinafores before walking the six miles to the show. There were nine children, and the exhibits and their bases would be brought home in the pram on top of the baby. One year someone moved grandad's tray of vegetables off the table at the flower show at Earl Soham just for devilment, grandad was so cross that he said he would never show again. He didn't, and there was never another show in that village because grandad always put in so many entries they no longer had enough to make up a show without him.

One day when I came home from school, mum told me that dad was changing his job and we were going to Cambridgeshire. Dad had not been feeling so well and the doctor had told him a change might do him good, so off we went to Bottisham, six miles from Cambridge to live in another tied cottage, in a long lane, three-quarters of a mile from the main road with no other children nearby to play with, only Ron and the two sisters I now had. But I was twelve by then and learning to help mother by doing such things as skin a rabbit and turn it into a stew, and to cook on the coal range we had in that house rather than the oil stove we had used in the other house.

I began to notice that dad seemed to be slow in doing his jobs and that when he sat down in his chair at night he slept much more than he had done. Mum suggested that I should drop in on the farm on my way home from school and give dad a hand. I went at weekends too and soon saw that he sometimes had trouble opening doors and picking things up. Then one weekend, I went round to the cowshed where I expected to find dad with the one old cow the farmer kept. To my horror, I found dad had fallen off the milking stool and the old cow had got her foot in the pail. Dad called to me to help him up and made me promise not to tell anyone he had fallen, he also asked me if I thought I could milk the cow. You can imagine how I felt to see my father, half crying in his despair. I realised that he must be ill, and for his sake I tried to milk the wretched animal. That first time I wasn't much good, but after a little while I got the hang of it, and from then on I used to go and do the milking before and after school.

But dad had, in the meantime been to the doctor and tests were being made as to why he could no longer grip things and why he was slowing up in all his movements. One day I came home to find mum in tears. Dad had been given the sack. He had had a terrible row with his boss who had found out that I had been doing the milking. Now what were we going to do? They searched the papers for jobs, but I think mum knew that it was going to be a struggle with dad as ill as he was. As luck would have it, they saw an advertisement for a farm worker on the very farm at Hoo where dad had started and where he had continued for twenty or more years. Mum wrote to the farmer explaining how things were with dad, and fortunately for us he replied that he was willing to give dad a try. So once again we packed our belongings on to the cattle lorry and back we came to Suffolk, to a very small cottage, far too small for a family with four children, but it was home.

I managed to get myself a weekend job at the same farm

cleaning out chicken huts and other odd jobs which was a help. During this time dad had to go to a London hospital for more tests, but one weekend, for no reason at all, it seemed to us, he fell off his bicycle. I told mum I thought he wasn't fit to cycle anymore, and from that day on he never rode it again. It was then that mum told me he had Parkinson's Disease. I had no idea how bad this was, but I soon did, as dad had to give up work and of course, we were faced with the prospect of being homeless for the cottage went with the job. Poor mum was beside herself with worry, but she went to see the local Pastor who was also a local Councillor and told him all our worries. Eighteen months later we heard that we had been allocated a Council house in Charsfield. The same day we heard that grandad had died, dad had so wanted him to know that we had finally got a house, but our good news came just too late.

Our new house had three large bedrooms, a large living room, a small front room and a big kitchen with a pantry. The bathroom had still got a copper in it which you had to light a fire beneath to get hot water, but that didn't worry mum. We were all delighted with our new house and as mum said "Peg, we are safe now as long as we pay our rent and keep our noses clean. We can stay here as long as we like."

There's an old saying, 'New house, new baby,' and it was not long after we had moved that mum took me aside to break the news that she was expecting a baby. Although dad was ill, the news made the whole family very happy. It meant however, that I had to help mum more and more around the house and there were times when the School Attendance Officer came to call to find out why I had been missing School. Mum never ever complained, however tired or overworked she was. Sometimes as dusk fell, or on a fine evening she'd say "Come on Peg, let's go out for a bit of air," and we would take a walk around the village.

My second brother was born in October 1950. I well remember dad waking me about five in the morning with the words, "Peg, you will have to go for the nurse." We were lucky in those days to have a midwife living in the village. The first job I did when I got back from calling her was to light the copper fire to get plenty of hot water. Then it was time to get the others up, fed and off to school. Between us dad and I looked after mum and the rest of the family, though we also had help from very good neighbours. Mum was up within a week, but kept pretty busy with the new baby, so as by this time dad was too shaky to shave himself, I learnt to do this for him, as well as lending him a hand with washing and dressing.

I had left school by this time and was working at the post office and general stores in the village. With my first week's wages I bought a high-tension battery for our radio for dad's one pleasure was listening to the wireless.

A year or so later, mum started going out to work in the fields helping with the fruit picking and any other work that came along. Dad kept an eye on the baby and the other three were at school. Mum was very glad of the few extra shillings she could earn, but on one occasion an official called from the National Assistance Board to check if mum really was working when she was claiming assistance. How my poor old dad kept his temper I don't know, he soon told the man that he supposed mum went out to work in the fields for the fun of it, then he got the National Assistance book and threw it across the table at the man telling him we didn't need their charity. Poor mother was so upset when she came in and heard all about it. Apparently she had worked more hours that was allowed to people claiming benefit, but what hurt her most was that someone must have reported her to the office. That made her very bitter.

But things did get a little easier at home. I went to a better paid job in Framlingham and Ron left school and started work too. I was growing up and started going out and about with other young people, but I had to be home by 10 o'clock. If I wanted to go to a dance I had to be in by 11.30, and it was a rare treat to be out until midnight.

COURTSHIP AND MARRIAGE

The Christian marriage has great meaning for me. As the good book says, "For this cause shall a man leave his mother and father and they shall become one flesh."

My story with Ernie is quite simple really and things seemed to follow a very natural course. I met him when I was 16 1/2 years old on a Church Choir Outing. Ernie, who was ten years older than me, was one of the group which used to meet on Sunday afternoons after church to go for a cycle ride to Woodbridge and then down to the river. We started cycling home together and then we used to meet sometimes in the churchyard where he had a part-time job tidying up the graves and I worked as a church cleaner. We often sat on the tombstones and talked. Ernie had been in lodgings most of his life as his mother had died when he was eighteen months old, and his landlady pulled his leg about me, saying that he was a kidnapper.

The first time we went out officially was to the Harvest Festival service at Dallinghoo and Ernie took me afterwards to have coffee with his brother and sister-in-law. After that we started going out three times a week and then I brought Ernie home to have tea. Dad was very pleased as he had always liked Ernie whom he had met at church. Mum thought I was a bit young to be 'goin steady' with a chap but she liked Ernie and soon made him welcome.

Ernie said there was quite a bit of jealousy from the other boys. Mind you, it was never mischievous. They just cheered and teased at dances, trying to 'excuse' us when we were dancing by cutting in on him, or they would try to date me. Not that anyone ever succeeded, Ernie was the only man for me.

Of course, in our day there were not many cars about, so we

did our courting by bicycle. During the winter we met on Sundays, Tuesdays, Thursdays and Saturdays in the evening. In the summer Ernie had several jobs in the village doing gardening as well as the churchyard job. Often I would help him by raking grass up, or hedge cutting. And it was in the churchyard where I learnt to fill in a grave. On Sunday we would meet at morning service, and then again at 2 p.m. to cycle to Woodbridge to meet friends and perhaps have a game of clock golf, and then we would cycle back for evening service. Sometimes we were in for a treat and it might be that we had a lantern service, with a visiting speaker, perhaps a missionary, illustrating his talk with slides projected onto a sheet. Then if it was summer, we might well cycle back to Woodbridge just to have a walk along the river wall. We also had a tandem and on this we took ourselves to the Speedway at Foxhall. We cycled miles around Suffolk on this machine and years later we added a side-car in which to put our first baby.

It was to Woodbridge too that we went for the Pictures. The cinema was known in those days as the 'flea-pit' but we often went in the more expensive seats which cost 2/6. On these trips we used to leave our cycles at the pub so we could call in for a shandy on the way home, but we always stood in the passageway as it was not considered the thing at all for a young girl to go into a pub, and in any case I was only seventeen.

Later we took dancing lessons so twice a week we would have to cycle to Wickham Market. Occasionally we would go to a Whist Drive, but whatever we were doing or wherever we had been, I still had to be in by 10.30 p.m. When we arrived at the back door, Ernie used to laugh and say that my mother gave us five minutes to say good night. Then, sure enough, the door would open and she would say, "Time you were going Ernie. You both have to get up early." I don't know what the young people of today would say to that. Nowadays, they have their cars to go where they like and most seem to have plenty of money, but for all that, they don't seem to be happy. We didn't have much but we made ourselves content with what we had.

In 1952 I went as a nursing auxiliary at St. Audry's

Psychiatric Hospital. It was hard work, but I enjoyed it and doing shift work meant that there were times when I could give mum a hand at home as she had been overdoing things. She suffered with bad legs and the fact that she had been cutting down apple trees three miles away and carting wood didn't help them much.

That Christmas, Ernie asked mum if we could get engaged. Mum and dad were pleased and so we planned the wedding for 6th June 1953. When Ernie proposed he said that for him it had been love at first sight. He said I was just what he'd dreamed of, a good old Suffolk girl who could not only cook but could turn her hand to anything. He knew that I would always help him, and he felt that we would make a good team. Ernie wanted, more than anything in the world, a proper home of his own. As for me, I new the value of a good and happy home, something Ernie had never had, for although times had been hard for us, my parents had always shown us love and affection, and I longed to make my own home. What's more, Ernie was so kind and we had lots of fun together, and although I had gone out a couple of times with two other chaps, they weren't a patch on Ernie.

Our wedding at St. Peter's Church, Charsfield, was a typical country affair. I wore a beautiful white dress that I borrowed from a nursing colleague and my two sisters and two of Ernie's nieces were bridesmaids. Their dresses were made for them as a present from one of mum's friends. As I walked up the aisle, not only did I feel like a million dollars, but my happiness was completed because my dear old dad was able to give me away.

Mum worked very hard to give me the best possible reception she could, but like most brides, I can't remember much about it now. Not like the reception we had for my son's wedding. There was a sort of horseshoe shape in the village hall filled with food. The rest of the table was just heads of roses and dahlias and I'd interwoven all the tables down the middle with Virginia Creepers. To eat there was soup, cold ham, turkey and different sorts of salad and gateaux. To drink there was my home-made wine. It doesn't look or taste that strong, but by the time the meal was finished ..! Now usually at a wedding the bride's guests are on one side and the groom's on the other, but by the time that they had found out that gooseberry and gorse was their favourite, they didn't know whose relations were who, or who they were having conversations with. They were on the table, under the table, or just plain flat out!

After our wedding Ernie and I went to live in Hoo. Ernie had changed his job for one that had a house with it, but he had arranged that he could still retain the job of grave digger in Charsfield. Our little cottage was very like the one in which I had been born in Easton, and in fact, it too had been part of the Duke of Hamilton's estate. Even in 1953 there was still no electricity or water laid on, but Calor gas supplied the cooker and a couple of lights. The toilet was an outside one, and our water came from a bore which had to be pumped from the farm.

The first thing we did was to paint all the woodwork white, except in the kitchen which we did in light green. Mum helped me to wallpaper the bedrooms. Ours had pink paper with tiny roses on it, the second bedroom we did in blue striped paper, and the third room we did not touch until I was expecting our first baby, and then mum came and put up a paper with a nursery pattern. In later years mum taught me how to hang wallpaper. Our furniture we thought was very good. I remember that when we married I had only saved £50, and Ernie spent £150 on the new furniture. I thought he was very rich! We had a new bedroom suite which included a dressing table, tallboy and wardrobe and a wooden bed with an interior sprung mattress which had just come into fashion. There was brown lino on the floor and pink mats, I even had two pink candlesticks. The second room was slightly smaller and in here we had a four-foot bed with a feather mattress given us as a wedding present by one of my aunts. The small dressing table and chest of drawers in this room were given us as a wedding present by my brother Ron. They had cost fifteen pounds which was a lot of money in those days. On the landing we just had another chest of drawers.

The front room downstairs was 12' x 10' and had a brick fireplace, and a Calor gas light. The walls were papered in pale green and there was lino on the floor. We had a new dining room suite and a glass cabinet that had been a wedding present. Later we did sugar beet hoeing and bought a three-piece suite with the proceeds.

The kitchen led off from this room. Next to a small open fireplace stood the Calor gas cooker in the corner. The old brick oven had been removed and the Calor gas cylinders stood in the other corner. The small sink had a single cold water tap. A white deal kitchen table, a couple of chairs and two small armchairs completed the furniture in here. The floor was covered in coconut matting overlaid with a rag rug. Later we added a kitchen dresser and later still a pram! Sometimes you could hardly move in here, let along swing a cat.

I do miss the pantry I had there, it was like a small room where you could walk right in, with shelves on each side. Usually the pantry was built on the north or east side of the house so things stored in there kept beautifully cool. We had a wire meat safe in one corner and large wooden flour bins, as flour was bought by the hundredweight then. I still buy mine by the stone from the local miller. The shelves of the pantry would be full of jars of jam and marmalade, bottles of fruit, pickles, red cabbage, onions, chutneys, jars of salted runner beans and pickled beetroot. Then there would be two or three Christmas puddings, the ones left over from the last making which you put by for the following year. Then too, there would be four to six different cake tins containing such things as a loaf cake, a sponge sandwich, rusks, buns and sausage rolls. On the floor stood the large brown stone pot where we kept the bread, the top always covered with a cloth. Next to this might be the bowl with the eggs in. Strange now to think that we used to preserve eggs to last through the winter. We used to do it like this. We bought a tin of water-glass from the ironmonger and then melted the contents with about a gallon of boiling water. When it had cooled, a wire basket was put into it and the next day we started putting the surplus eggs into it.

40

They would keep for up to six months like this, the only drawback was that the liquid turned into a white jelly-like consistency and you would have to feel about to find the eggs.

I was very happy in this cottage. We worked hard on the garden and even had two pigs in the pigsty at the bottom of the garden as well as one hundred chickens. I always said that if I had the money I would have had a small farm. Our garden was our hobby. We had the best cabbages and cauliflowers ever and we always maintained that it was where we used to empty the closet pail that the best greens grew.

In those early years I also went out to work on the fields, fruit picking, chopping beet and so on. I still went home when I could to give mum a hand helping to wash and look after dad. I had two miscarriages during this time but eventually, after a very difficult pregnancy, our son Allan was born in August 1957.

We had been at Hoo for six and a half years when one day Ernie came home from work and said that he had had enough. He didn't see eye to eye with his boss, so he started looking for a new job. I was pretty fed up too with the water situation, it was so brown. I used to fill baths and buckets at night in the hope that by the next morning the brown sediment had settled. It was quite a pantomime when we had a bath. First we had to heat the water in the portable copper which Ernie had bought me and which stood in the shed. Then we filled the bath placed in front of the fire. After the bath, you had to put on a dressing gown and go down the garden to empty the bath.

A promising job for Ernie was advertised in the local paper, it was for a stockman at an experimental farm near Ipswich. He applied, went for an interview and got the job. I was most impressed when I saw the cottage that went with the job, there was a proper bathroom, and not only was electricity laid on, there was a gas main as well. The garden was an awful mess, but that didn't worry us. What did was how I would break the news to my mum. Dad was getting worse, unable now to feed himself, and I had been going to see them every other day. I used to go on my cycle, holding on with one hand while I

41

pulled the pram with the other.

We sold our pigs and chickens, packed up and moved to our new home on a main road. It took time to get used to the traffic, but I celebrated by having the biggest wash ever, I was so pleased to have running water and no more brown stains. Not only was there running water on tap, there was hot water, as there was a back boiler in the fireplace. I did miss my old copper though, I do like to give my wash a good boil to get it really white. I'm old fashioned I know.

The soil in our new garden was very light so we had to put plenty of mulch on it. We had a battle against that common weed, Fat-hen, which will take over the place if you're not careful. The garden and the adjoining field were full of it. The surrounding country was very open and at first I missed the trees and hedges, and when the wind blew it was like a desert with dust everywhere and the soil blowing across the fields.

Ernie had been taken on as a pigman, so you can tell how we felt when we heard that the farm was selling off all its pigs. The Farm Manager told him that he would have to take on the job of cowman. This worried Ernie because, being an experimental farm, each cow had a special record to be kept, and not being much of a scholar, Ernie thought he would not be able to cope with this side of things. But he said he would give it a try, especially as in November 1959 I had given birth to our second son, David. But he did not like the work and told the farm manager so, who just turned round and gave him the sack. He had an awful temper that man, and was just like an Army sergeant. Ernie came home very upset and was so fed up with life on the land that the following week he went off to Woodbridge and got himself a Council job on the roads. It was rather strange as my brother Ron had also left the land and gone to work for the Council.

At the time Ernie left the land it was quite a common thing for men to give up farming. Wages were poor and they found they could earn much more in factories or on building sites, but you had to remember that when you left the land, you left your home as well. So our next task was to see the Council Housing

Officer to see if we could get a Council house. I was beside myself with worry because the Farm Manager had called on me to say that if we didn't get out of the farm's house, he would have us evicted and the children would be put in a home. I went again to the Council, but there seemed no prospect of any house becoming vacant. Then Ernie was served with a Court Order for possession of the house, but five days before we were due to go we heard we had been allocated a house on an estate at Kesgrave. We were not over happy at the idea of living on a big estate, but we knew that as long as we could pay our rent we would be safe. So in January of 1961 we moved with all our house plants and shrubs, and prepared to settle down, but as it happened, within six months we were on the move again. This time back to Charsfield.

Mum had heard that a house was becoming empty in the village. I think she was hoping that if we got back to Charsfield I could help her with the nursing of my father. We put in for an exchange and moved just at the time when the beans and peas in the Kesgrave garden were nearly ready to pick. We had to leave them, but we did dig up all the rose bushes and wrapped them in plastic sacks as they were in full bud. People said we would lose them, but we dug a trench to put them in and left them until the autumn when we set them into their permanent beds. The first thing my husband had to do in this garden was mow the grass down, as the garden was in an awful mess.

It was nice to be back in the village. Although this house was not as good as the one in Kesgrave, we felt this was home and we hoped it would be our last move. It was an older house and didn't have a bathroom, though it did have a flush toilet. The sitting room and the kitchen were large and there was a good pantry and three decent sized bedrooms. Ernie got busy with the garden and it wasn't long before we had a chicken run and twelve more chickens. Our next-door neighbour was a very good old gardener and he used to talk to us and tell us about the land and give good advice about planning it all out, and we spent every moment we could getting it turned over and putting plenty of muck into it.

Well, that's a short history of the early part of our life, and if you want me to be more specific and chronological than that, then it's a hard task, for the most chronological I'll ever get in that sense, is to use the word chronological! You see, when I look back on my marriage, I don't see it as a series of events, but as a long path with little tracks leading off and back on to it. Ernie and I had the same interests, which counts for a lot. Now whether that's because living a relatively simple life in the country, you can't help having the same interests, I don't know. Perhaps in the cities where everything is more complicated, then it's harder to find people whose thoughts are completely in tune with yours, but we were like that, often one of us saying something and the other answering, "Well I'll be darned, I was just going to say that." I find that rather strange and wonderful, but then, we also worked at our marriage. Very often we've toiled in our garden, carting muck in the pouring rain, slithering about in a squelchy mud, or sweating in the heat of a summer's day, or battling against strong winds to save our plants, when we might have preferred to be indoors with our feet up, but we did it together - we were, what we set out to be when we made our marriage vows, a partnership.

Sadly, that partnership was broken after thirty years, when, early one morning in May 1980, Ernie died in his sleep at my side. He was a dear, sweet man and as much a part of me as the air we breathe. We had never had a row, not a real row, just the occasional sharp word, but that was soon forgotten for Ernie was the salt of the earth, a man for whom the simple things of life mattered most, and as I work in the lovely garden that we created together, I feel nearer to him than in any other place, and for me Ernie will live on not only in my thoughts but in the beauty and colours of our garden.

*Clay Jones, Peggy Cole and Geoff Hamilton
filming for 'Gardener's World'*

THE GARDEN

It was in 1970 that Allan's and David's Commander of the St. John Ambulance Brigade, the late Major Schreiber, called to see us to ask if we would consider opening our garden to the public to help in their fund raising. Ernie's and my immediate reaction to this was to wonder what people would say. Would they think we were getting a bit above ourselves and say things like, "Who ever do they think they are, opening a Council house garden!" Then, when we'd given it a great deal of thought, we decided, well why not, provided the Council don't mind. So we asked for and got the Council's permission and then waited.

On that day in July 1970 the garden was open for the first time and never, ever did it cross our minds that five hundred people would turn up to look at our garden. We were amazed, to say the least, for people had come, not just from the immediate area, but from all over the place. The following year we decided to open it again for one Sunday. But then we had had folk calling during the week saying they were sorry but they couldn't come on that particular Sunday, but could they just have a look round. That made us have a really good think. It seemed to us that we could help raise some money for the church, so we decided that weather permitting we would have the garden open from the middle of July until the end of September.

And that's what we have done ever since. You may ask why so many people should want to come and look at a Council house garden. I think it is to see what can be done without paid help, and also to see just how self-sufficient we are on our third of an acre. (At one time we had a bit more as our neighbour at the time found that he had more than he could cope with, so we cultivated part of his land as well.)

46

Our land is a mixed soil, heavy at the back of the house and light at the front. The plot is shaped like the letter 'L'. Sloping down to the road from the front of the house is four feet of embankment on which I have African Marigolds. They seem to stick the heat very well as it gets very hot in that spot in the summer. At the top of the embankment, where previously have stood dwarf conifers, I have now planted Berberis (Thumbergii - Darts Purple), and in beds near the front door are 80 mixed roses. On the left of the path is the rockery, then passing the garage you come to a small fishpond with a waterfall and a waterwheel which is surrounded by more rockery and lawn, edged with herbaceous borders. As you reach the backyard you will see sinks with the herbs in, and a small rose bed edged with pots full of Cacti, Fuchsias, Geraniums and Hostas. From my kitchen window I look out at Honeysuckle, Ceanothus, Everlasting Sweet Peas and Clematis. These are all grown up the sides of the sheds to try to hide the walls.

I think we owe a lot of our initial success in the garden to our old neighbour who died in 1965. He was a wonderful old character, and when we first moved in, he gave us some very good advice about such things as to which bit of the garden was best for which crops. Whenever I went into the garden, there he would be in his, with a hoe in his hand. You'd never find a weed in his garden, his favourite expression was "Keep the hoe going". He was very wise on country matters, I once saw him kill a mole with his gun and he knew exactly at what moment to shoot into the soil.

As you continue up the garden you pass on the left two greenhouses, one is 19' x 10', the other 8' x 10'. The larger one is used for raising all the bedding plants as it is heated. I raise between two and three thousand plants a year, and also grow many pot plants. When the season for bedding plants is over, we take the shelves out from one side and use the area for growing tomatoes and cucumbers. Alternate years the smaller greenhouse is used for melons, peppers and sometimes more cucumbers.

Passing the greenhouses you come to my new layout of more

herbaceous borders with a new lawn and shrubs. This part is cut off from the vegetable garden by climbing roses - Schoolgirl, Handel, and Parkdirektor Riggers. Still on the left as we near the top of the garden is the spot where each year I used to grow 80 to 100 Dahlias and about 100 Chrysanthemum plants followed by 80 odd Gladioli corms, this plot is now used to grow dried flowers for my arrangements. I have only one apple tree on this side of the garden a Bramley Seedling, a real good cooker that is. We have had hundredweights of fruit off this tree. Then there is the asparagus bed, and next to that the vines which climb all over the three sheds in which we keep the seed trays and flower pots, use another as a wood store and the third for all the garden tools.

Since 1992 we have expanded the garden by another quarter of an acre. Our neighbour kindly sold us a piece of his orchard, this has made a big difference to our visitors, as we have three large picnic benches and other seats. People do just like to sit and while their time away. We have left it as an orchard, with fourteen Bramley Seedlings, plus the same number of plum trees, Warwickshire Drooper. We have also planted some Crabapple trees and soft fruit bushes, such as Loganberry and Tayberry on the outlaying boundary. Ronnie has also planted 2 cwt of mixed bulbs under the trees, this looks very pretty in the Springtime.

Starting back down the garden we have the chicken run. When the boys were young their pet the golden pheasant and his three wives also lived here. Apart from the chicken run, the entire right-handside of the garden is given over to vegetables. Before he died, Ernie and I used to get down to the job of working out our year's plan for the garden in December or January so that we could get in our orders for seed. We always bore in mind the principle that you must never grow the same things two years in succession on the same spot. If you do, you run the danger of say getting pea weevil if you plant peas on top of peas. You must rotate, otherwise the earth becomes sick, rather like a person who never changes his job or works too much on one thing. Mind you, like every rule, there are exceptions and you can keep an onion bed forever. We keep our plans from year to year so that we can work things out almost scientifically. It's not so important to vary the flowers, however. You soon get to know your land and what grows best where. One part of the land is much finer than the rest, so that we have for the smaller salad crops. Our aim is to try to create a soil which is a fine, crumbly mixture using plenty of farmyard muck or compost.

One other recent change has been made opposite the greenhouses, my brother dug me a pond, 18' x 10', with landscaping of rockery and herbaceous. Visitors spend much time sitting on the garden seat, watching the fish. I must admit I love to hear the water fountain, there is something very therapeutic about running water in a garden.

October is the time to start the job of clearing the land and digging in the manure before the frosts starts. When Ernie hurt his back pulling out a hedge, my brother Ron came to lend a hand with the digging, and bless his heart, he has continued to help me with the garden since Ernie passed away. So it is Ron who you would see now carting the muck and getting it well dug in. Also in October we pull up the old broad bean and dwarf bean plants, saving any seed we have left on, and we clean and tie up all the pea sticks and canes. Into the greenhouse go the pots of Cacti, Fuchsias and Geraniums, but not until I have given the whole place a wash down with Jeyes Fluid (1 teaspoon to a gallon of water), and put polythene sheeting up inside to help keep it a bit warmer. I do have an electric tube heater but I keep this at only just above freezing point to keep plants free from frost. This month too we help a neighbour pick the apples off his five acre orchard, and in our garden we plant out spring cabbages.

In November I get the Dahlias up, cut the tops off and wash the tubers in Jeyes Fluid, dry them off thoroughly on the bench in the greenhouse. If you don't do this you stand a chance of mildew setting in and rotting them. Another job for this month is to get up all the Chrysanthemum stools and box them ready to take cuttings in February or early March. I also tidy up the herbaceous borders and have a good old bonfire with all the rubbish. Then I lift the Gladioli and cut the tops off the asparagus before giving the bed a really good mulch with muck. Now is the time to plant four or five rows of broad beans and a couple of rows of shallots, as well as planting out the rest of the Stocks, Sweet Williams and Wallflowers. It is also time to dig a new runner bean trench.

December is always a busy month, made slightly easier for me now as I no longer go turkey plucking, but still the Christmas decorations and everything else, but come Boxing Day I'm out in the greenhouse planting onion seed, Robinson Mammouth and Kelsae. Most of the small seed I raise using heat from a 60 watt electric light bulb in a box under the seed box. I find this much better than trying to heat the whole greenhouse.

During the first week in January we get off our orders from the seed catalogues. If the weather is right we are probably still doing a bit of digging and carting in the manure. It certainly keeps us fit bringing in about twenty barrow loads of it and pushing it all up the slope into the garden. Time too to dig up the rest of the parsnips, leaving them to lie on the top of the land for a bit to get the frost. We also take a look at the carrots and beetroot which we store in sand in the second, unheated greenhouse.

While the menfolk get on with things like checking and repairing the seed boxes I shut myself away in the greenhouse to start to cut down the Fuchsias and Geraniums. I put the Dahlia tubers in boxes of peat and sand to start them off for cuttings. Chrysanthemums are also started off this way. Another thing I do is to sow red cabbage, cabbage, cauliflower and lettuce seed. I find that the cabbages sown now, quickly catch up the spring cabbage which we planted in October. This might be a good place to tell you about some of the things I have in the greenhouse later in the year when the bedding plants have been moved out. At one end I have a lovely blue climbing shrub called Plumbago. Then, as I am very fond of variegated plants, I have many varieties of Coleus. I must have about a hundred varieties of Fuchsia in and around the greenhouse. Someone once asked me if I ever counted the varieties of flowers in the garden. I told them that I knew there were over a thousand, but I couldn't be sure of all the names. But I can tell you that I have got Ferns, Impatients (Busy Lizzie), Hypoestes (Polka Dot Plant), Cyclamens, Gloxinias, Achimenes (Hot Water Plant) and many kinds of Geraniums all giving the beauty of their different colours to my greenhouse.

February is seed sowing time for Antirrhinums, Salvias, Lobelia, Petunias and tomatoes and by the end of the month I shall have sown all my flower seeds. Then we prick out the onions, cabbages, lettuces and so on, and if at all possible we put in the first of the peas, radish, parsnips and four more rows of broad beans. Assuming that the land is fit to get on, we also try now one row of early potatoes, covering them with cloches, and two more rows of shallots. It is also time to fill in the runner bean trench.

Rose pruning and a tidying up in the herbaceous beds are two jobs that should be done in March. The lawns have their first cut and we start planting more peas, carrots, lettuce, turnips and spinach. Under cloches we put two rows of French beans. Towards the very end of the month I plant out the Gladioli and Pansies and the Sweet Pea plants. In the greenhouse I sow the last of the flower seeds, Zinnias, French Marigolds and African Marigolds. I also try to start marrows, cucumbers and runner beans in pots so that I have something for the early shows, but you have to be very lucky not to get them caught by the frost. If there is a frost warning, we cover them up with newspaper, but I don't put them out in the garden until the first week in April.

Once we have cleared the land of the old Brussels Sprout plants and dug over any spare land, then April is the time for getting in the rest of the potatoes, the beetroot seed and more carrots and peas. By now my greenhouse is pretty well jam-packed with boxes of seedlings and most days I'm hard at it pricking out. It is the time too to water the Cacti, Old wives' tale or not, I sow parsley seed this month in the greenhouse. I am very fond of this herb and I always pour boiling water on the seed to start it off, then when it is big enough to prick out, I transplant it first into boxes and then out into the garden, putting it between the onions because it is supposed to keep the greenfly away. In the nursery bed we plant all the varieties of the cabbage family during the first few days of April. As soon as I can, I get some of the flower plants out of the greenhouse and into the garden frame in order to leave room for me to take half of the staging down on one side and get the early tomato plants straight into the ground.

May is planting-out time. I put the Dahlia tubers out early, hoping that I can escape the frost, as by this time the tubers have as much as four or five inches of growth on them. Marrows and sweetcorn go out too, as do my special onions. Hanging baskets should also be ready to go out. I like to make up baskets with hanging Geraniums (Lilac Gem) and Pendula Lobelia (Sapphire). Another favourite of mine is a basket with three plants of the Fuchsia called La Campanella. Other lovely ones for baskets that I have used are Golden Marinka, Lakeside, Wings of Song and Cascade. It usually takes me a couple of weeks to plant out all my bedding plants and then there are the odd boxes, pots and wheelbarrows which we plant up with Fuchsia and Geranium. We used to try to get to the Chelsea Flower Show this month, over the years however, the high cost of rail fares made this too expensive, this time was then spent by planting the outdoor Chrysanthemums, potting up about a dozen late ones so I had flowers in late autumn, and putting out the cucumbers into the cold greenhouse. But now as a journalist I am lucky enough to attend the 'Press Day' at the Show, and this has become the highlight of my year.

Surprisingly, we can get some very strong winds in June so now is the time to make sure that you have your sticks in with the peas and the Dahlias and the Gladioli are well staked. By now there will be a lot of growth in the herbaceous border so watch out for the slugs. A good going round with the spray gun filled with Jeyes Fluid (again 1 teaspoon to the gallon of water) on the roses, cabbages and peas is a wise precaution. Your hoe, as our neighbour used to say, should be on the go the whole time, both to destroy the weeds and put air into the soil. I also start now to feed my exhibition onions with the juice taken from the tank that has a sack of muck soaking in it. As a general fertiliser I use Phostrogen. As the weather gets warmer we mulch the runner beans, we dead head the Dahlias and I start once more making up a compost heap with all my waste material. You would be surprised what goes into that heap!

During July we just keep things ticking over, watering when we can, especially in the greenhouse perhaps twice a day. The tomatoes need side shooting and tidying up, and the Dahlias disbudding for preparation for early shows.

I think of August as the month when I am busy reaping the benefit of all our hard work as I set about freezing all the surplus vegetables and fruit. Cauliflowers, beans, carrots and new potatoes all freeze well and I reckon to have all our own vegetables on Christmas Day to serve with one of our own cockerels if I have fattened one, as well as home-made wine and puddings. Already in August there is a hint in the air of starting to plan for next year as we sow cabbage seed for next spring and lettuce seed for planting out in October. Then there are the Christmas bulbs to go into pots and Geranium cuttings to be taken. We lift our main crop of potatoes at the end of this month.

September is storing time. The onions are lifted and tied in bunches and hung up around the side of the shed. The apples are picked and put in trays in an apple rack, the carrots and beet are put in boxes of sand and peat. Then I start to clear the flower beds and plant Daffodil and Tulip bulbs and Polyanthus ready for the spring flowering. In the greenhouse I take out the old cucumber plants and in their place I plant lettuce seed. The leeks need earthing up and all the old yellow leaves should be taken off the Brussels Sprouts.

I could go on. When one has a garden there is always a job to be done. But I have tried to give you some idea of how we run

53

our garden. If you like I have given you our year in a nutshell, and a very tiny nutshell at that! Gardening to me is a never-ending joy, a close look at God's creation and the enjoyment there is to be had from it.

By-the-way, I no longer have my old home-made propagator. I'm up to date now, with a new modern one, complete with temperature settings!

A FEW TIPS FOR THE GARDEN

This book is not a Gardening Manual, in fact, I suppose you could say that with the little bit of everything that I'm putting in, it's more like the good old-fashioned stock pot, or if you would prefer a sweeter comparison, what about a pot-pourri, that lovely mixture of all the sweet smelling petals of the summer which we preserve to give us pleasure in the winter. Now, having got the idea of sweet smells in your mind, I'm going to pass on the most important tip I can give you, and that is, if you want good soil then you must keep putting compost into it. Only peat and manure will get your soil right. It's just like making pastry, the more you keep rubbing the fat in, the more crumbly the consistency becomes. When people ask me why my plants grow so well, I tell them the answer really does lie in the soil, and in the same way that what goes up must come down, so what comes out must first have gone in.

Fertiliser and Compost

There are two types of fertiliser, the stuff you make yourself using all the waste products from the kitchen like vegetable peelings and the old plant material when it has finished its useful life, all of which goes on a heap somewhere at the top of the garden. Then there is chemical fertiliser, but in my opinion this is used far too much. I think that the farmers should mix their straw with silage and get it back into the ground rather than all this burning of stubble. And you know, there is no doubt in my mind that the vegetables and plants that have had artificial fertiliser on them are not as good. Potatoes, in particular, can have very big blotches on them and when you cook them they go very watery. So we stick to the use of organic matter, for we know that can't harm us.

In my grandfather's and even my father's day, the compost heap was a big hole at the top of the garden into which they put all their rubbish to rot down. A pail used to stand outside the back door and into this went all the household 'chates' - tea leaves, vegetable peelings and so on, all of which was tipped on to the compost heap. Nowadays we make our compost more scientifically. Ours, which is between two of our sheds, is a box-like structure (4' x 3') made of old corrugated tin. We start at the ground level spreading all the waste matter to form a layer. Most soft green stuff that will rot down can go in, but beware of potato peelings because they have a tendency to grow again, and old cabbage stalks take far too long to rot, so we stand ours up to dry and then I have a good bonfire and burn them. It is better to burn all diseased plant material, certainly you must never put this into the compost otherwise you will spread disease all over the garden.

Once you have got a good layer of green then, if you have any manure, now is the time to sprinkle some on the heap. We put our chicken droppings in. If manure is not available then sprinkle the heap with sulphate of ammonia at the rate of 1/2oz. to the square yard with 8 gallons of water. Any garden centre will advise you as to the proprietary brands which are available if you would rather not use the sulphate of ammonia. An inch of soil can also be thrown over the heap at this stage. It is a good idea to repeat this every 4 inches adding 4 ozs. of chalk or lime to the square yard to help break down and sweeten the compost. When you get to four feet start another heap, but do remember to water weekly if the weather is very hot and to turn the heap every 6 weeks

Seeds

I grow just about everything and most of it from seed, so it is vital that the conditions are right for sowing. The main thing to remember for outside sowing is that the land must be dry enough to allow treading without the soil clinging to your boots, what we call 'a loving soil'. Hoe or lightly fork over the ground to a depth of 2 to 3 inches to allow the soil to dry out thoroughly. All the large stones and rough clods are removed by raking, then the soil is firmed by treading with the feet and then raked over again to provide a fine tilth. Then you are ready to sow in the rows you have marked out using a line. Do remember too to sow thinly in the case of those vegetables that are going to be transplanted, and always grow a clump of extra beans at the end of the rows so that we can fill in any gaps after the birds have had a go! If the weather is very dry, water the seed bed before sowing.

For indoor sowing I start in February getting the seed trays ready in the greenhouse. I use compost reinforced soil rather than a peat based one as this does try out quickly and as I go out to work I am not always on hand to water. If the seeds do dry out, they will scorch. And do prick out as soon as the seedlings are big enough.

Pruning

Any good gardening book will give you details about pruning, but I just want to say a word here about how important it is to cut back woody plants such as roses, fruit trees and shrubs. There are three main objectives in pruning, to regulate growth, improve the quality of the flowers and fruit, and to remove damaged, diseased or dead wood. The removal of part of the top growth of a plant causes a reaction in the root system resulting in new stem growth. Damaged, dead or diseased shoots must be pruned back to healthy clean wood and this must be done before any other pruning is carried out. When you have finished cutting out the damaged parts you should paint any large wounds with a proprietary sealing compound to prevent disease spores entering the wounds. All pruning cuts should be made as cleanly as possible so as not to damage the plant cells. The timing of pruning is of great importance and it is essential to know the habits of trees and shrubs before starting to prune. As a general rule young roses, fruit trees and ornamental trees and shrubs are pruned hard at the time of planting, but I also cut my roses back hard each year and I find I get much better roses for this.

Hard Pruning

In this method you drastically cut back growing shoots to maybe within three or four dormant buds above ground level. Hard pruning of top growth helps the roots and encourages strong growth.

Light Pruning

This is shortening of laterals or leaders during early spring before the new growing season begins to encourage the development of flower buds or young shoots. The removal of dead flower heads is also classed as light pruning.

Winter Pruning

The main cutting back of deciduous trees, especially fruit trees should be done from November onwards. The severity of the pruning depends on the age of the trees. Newly planted trees require hard pruning to encourage strong growth. On established trees prune crowded lateral shoots and shorten leaders to maintain or improve the shape of the tree.

House Plants

My favourite are Fuchsias and Geraniums. What they need is warmth to start with in the early part of the year, and then later, as much air as possible, and they must not be allowed to dry out. You need to be careful about watering, it is so easy to overdo it. I like plants to sit on gravel which breaks up the moisture. A good guide is to put a piece of newspaper on the top of the soil in the flower pot. It should come away just wet. If it doesn't then it needs watering.

With Fuchsias, at the early part of growth you prick them out. Every little joint that comes out should be nipped out at the top to make the plant send out two shoots. Keep nipping out the tops and you will get a lovely busy plant. The same applies to Geraniums, so many people let their plants get too tall and leggy. Feeding of house plants is important. I use Phostrogen or liquid manure. Don't forget that house plants put outside for the summer need feeding too.

And I see nothing wrong in talking to plants. To me it seems the natural thing to do. When I go into the greenhouse, I am quite likely to say, "How are you today, my dears? It's a bit cold outside, but you cheer up because I want you to grow big and strong." I was once overheard doing this by one of my boys. Later he said "Mum, I know you work at the psychiatric hospital, but I didn't think you bought your work home with your!" But I didn't mind, I am sure that the plants feel your presence and sense your sympathy with them.

Slugs

I think slugs are the worst pest in the garden. There are proprietary baits available which will deal with most of them. My dad used to put barley chaff down beside the garden path. This is prickly stuff and the slugs did not like it. Neither do they like soot, so when you have your chimney swept put soot down one side of the garden. Another way to deal with them is to put hot lime in a powered form in an old sack and then just as it gets dusk and the ground is moist, shake the powder over their trails and on the ground around. It if rains you will need to repeat this.

AT THE SHOWS

Showing and Judging

Most flower shows still run successfully, the most noticeable change locally is Grundisburg, this used to be a big show, many of the old enthusiastic exhibitors have passed away, producing a decrease in the number of entries, and sadly the younger generation do not seem keen to carry on the traditions, this has greatly reduced the size of the annual show.

I am kept busy most Saturdays in July and August, but I do now find myself having to turn down travelling long distances to shows as time is very precious to me, and also I do not like leaving my brother alone to cope with all the visitors to the garden. We more often than not have coach parties arrive on Saturdays, and the people visiting do like to meet me.

So I am busy either exhibiting or judging, and over the years we have covered many thousands of miles doing this. Ernie didn't like showing, but I persuaded him to help me with the judging in the last few years of his life. We had both of us, some years ago, attended Evening Classes at Otley Agricultural College, which were a tremendous help to us. To become a judge, for two years I went as a student judge with various well established judges from whom I learned much, though I am particularly grateful to the late Mr H. Boreham, who taught me more than I can ever say. He was, both a wonderful judge and a very down-to-earth man.

I think there must be very few females who judge vegetables as so many show organisers looked surprised when I tell them that I have come to judge these for them. I like this work as I grow and show vegetables myself. I have won over a thousand prizes at local shows and well over fifty trophies, so I think that having spent many, many hours getting my own exhibits ready that I should know what to look for. I amaze myself now

Peggy Cole with trophies won at the Woodbridge Flower Show

when I think of the Friday nights I have sat up all night and just managed to lie down for an hour as the dawn chorus started. One weekend I entered two shows which involved 90 exhibits, including wine and cookery, so I had to start getting things ready at the beginning of the week. Mind you it was well worth it, for at the end of the shows I took home four trophies and seventy prizes.

July is the month for the flower shows. Ipswich has the first big show of the season and is well known for its roses and floral arrangements. Grundisburg, is especially good for its cookery class, Woodbridge seems to fall down with entries of roses but is good for Sweet Peas and also gains top marks for its floral arrangements. Kesgrave excels for its wine - in some shows there are over 800 bottles, and they also have a very good autumn show of Dahlias and Chrysanthemums. Hadleigh, over the years has become well known for its Suffolk Onion and Leek Championship. Eye, Felixstowe, Debenham, Bildeston, Framlingham, Melton and Wickham Market all have very good shows, but as I go round I still think Orford Show takes a lot of beating. It is always held on August Bank Holiday Saturday with 800 or more entries and I have yet to see carrots or parsnips beat the ones at Orford, they can be as long as my arm.

There is always a marvellous atmosphere in the hall or marquee where a show is being held; the air is heavy with the scent of the flowers as well as the smell of the earth and a sense of endeavour. Everyone is deeply involved in their own affairs, and there is a great air of secrecy, with damp cloths covering many of the exhibits, awaiting the right moment to reveal to the world some prized specimen. No one ever says anything, but when you go back in the afternoon after the judging has taken place, there are some long faces, I can tell you. Now this is where I like to see good sportsmanship. I mean, if you've lost, well then, I think to myself, there's always another year, and I must try harder for the next time.

When preparing to enter for a show, do make sure you read the schedule carefully. I know that sounds obvious, but you would be surprised at how many people can come a cropper at this stage. I have myself. I once put nine pods of peas in at one show when it should have been twelve.

Regretfully, because of time, I now only exhibit at the shows in my own village, and sadly also, over the years I have developed arthritis, this can be very painful at times, especially in my knees and hip. Leg ulcers also trouble me, but like I have said many times, 'Once out in the garden you try to forget the pain.'

On a happier note, my name has become well known, so I do get asked to open fetes and flower shows, sometimes though I have to say 'no', or I could be out every weekend in the summer months. It is nothing to be booked up some eighteen months to two years ahead.

Other honours I currently enjoy, I am President, both at Ipswich Horticultural Flower Show and Ipswich Co-op Horticultural Show.

I hope that the following few tips will be of interest to you, over the years they have helped me to win.

VEGETABLES

Potatoes

Wash each one carefully with a sponge dipped in a little milk. Put under a wet cloth, then when dry wrap in tissue paper and keep under several layers of newspapers, making sure that you don't let the daylight get to them as this quickly turns them green.

Peas

These should be picked off with scissors in order not to damage the calyx and do try to leave the waxy bloom on the pea. I always hold mine up to the light to check how many peas are in the pods and to see if there are any maggots!

Broad Beans

These offer very little scope, so all you can do is again cut with scissors and try to arrange neatly. Too often people just put them on the table, stick a number of them and leave them.

Cauliflowers

They must be white, not yellow and certainly not brown. If a cauliflower looks good in the week before the show, pick off the outside leaves and lay them over the top of the cauliflower to keep its colour.

Tomatoes

Always show with the calyx left on.

Collection Tray

Try to arrange your collection in order of points:-

e.g.		
Potatoes	20 Points
Runner Beans	18 Points
Tomatoes	18 Points
Parsnips	20 Points
Onions	20 Points
Cauliflowers	20 Points
Peas	20 Points
Leeks	20 Points
Celery	20 Points
Carrots	20 Points
Cucumber	20 Points

French Beans and Runner Beans

First pick with scissors, then wrap in damp paper. I then wrap mine in an old damp cloth which helps to keep them straight. Sometimes, if you do it carefully, it is possible to bend a bean straight. Of course, the most important thing is to make sure that the beans are young ones.

Carrots

Leave these till last. Lift them and wash only with cold water, keeping the foliage, then put them in a damp cloth. The top of the carrot should not have any green on it, this is caused by exposure when growing, so cover the soil as they grow to prevent this. Carrots soon lose their colour if left in the light.

Onions
This is one of my favourite vegetables for showing. I don't know why, but so many people spoil their exhibits by peeling off all the outside skins. This should never be done. Again, take the trouble to arrange your exhibit nicely on the stand.
Shallots

Here is something you can prepare in advance. They should all be of an even size and tied down at the neck to look like miniature onions. They look best if you can stand them in a pot of sand.

Red Beet

Globe beet will develop two weeks before long beet. Be careful when lifting not to break the tap root as this will lead to bleeding and will lose you marks on the show bench. Wash the beet in cold water and trim the side roots carefully. Pack in a damp cloth. Remember to leave the top leaves on.

Cabbages

These should be clean and have good hard centres.

Lettuces

Like cabbages they should be clean with a good centre. Lift with the root on and wash and wrap the root with a damp cloth and pop it all in a bag to keep the root damp.

Marrows

These do bruise easily, so take care how you pack for the show. You should display a matching pair.

Brussels Sprouts

Here a uniform size is required. Do not remove too many outer leaves otherwise the depth of colour is reduced.

Celery

I don't show this for the simple reason that we can't grow good enough specimens for show purposes. On our soil, the slugs always get to the celery before we do! But if you are showing, then tie each specimen below the foliage and lay it flat on the bench.

Cucumbers

Try to get completely matched pairs, with a nice dark colour and blossoms still attached. Again lay flat on the bench to display.

EXHIBITING FLOWERS

Flowers, like vegetables, need special care when being shown and being transported to the show. Roses must not be full blown, so I have been known to tie a piece of wool round the bud to stop it coming out too soon, or pick it on a Thursday and keep it in water in the 'fridge' until the last possible moment. I also cut Chrysanthemums at the beginning of the week and keep in a cold room, making sure that I have bruised the stems well, so that they can take up water. This tip also applies to all flowers with woody stems. Dahlias have to be picked very carefully as they bruise and mark very easily, so again they should be gathered in advance. You can use the wool tied round the flower technique on Gladioli too, but if your problem is the other way, and it looks as if they are not going to be open in time, then three or four days before the show, cut them and bring them into a warm room.

Stocks and Zinnias need to have the ends of their stems put on a hot plate or be dipped in boiling water for about three seconds, but a word of warning here, do be careful not to damage the blooms. I always wrap the heads in newspaper as a protection. Some flowers, like Poppies and Euphorbia, will bleed when their stems are cut and give off a milky fluid, so these too need to be sealed by burning. Sweet Peas also need careful picking the day before a show and should be put straight into cold water.

If you are doing floral arrangements then the foliage used must be thoroughly soaked. In our house if I have a show on Saturday, then no one can have a bath from Thursday evening onwards, as I need it for the more important job of giving all my foliage a jolly good soak. The flowers that I'm using are also picked on Thursday and put into a five-gallon drum, the flowers being plunged right up to their necks so that they too can have a good old drink. So many people make the mistake of picking flowers just before the flower show morning and very soon the leaves start to look tired, often before the judging has even started.

One final tip here, don't forget to take some spare blooms with you just in case one should get snapped off during the transporting of the exhibits. Don't let my milkman know, but I use an old milk crate to stand my vases in, but I also use old pillows, bricks, newspapers and various other wedges to help keep pots and vases upright in the car.

In some small shows the judges will automatically disqualify you if you have done something not according to the schedule, but Ernie and I didn't like doing that. I always try to leave a little note to tell the person what's gone wrong, and give them perhaps, a third prize. When we are judging flowers and vegetables we look first for uniformity, then for the way the item is presented. However good the vegetable may be, if it is just brought in and dumped down any old how on the bench, then it will lose marks.

THE COOKERY SECTION

I always enjoy judging cookery classes as I can taste all the exhibits on my way round! But there are formalities first, being met by whoever is running the show, then being taken into the hall for a complete walk round so that you can get an overall impression. From amongst the committee someone will act as steward and walk with you so that when you decide on your placings, they will actually put the 1st. 2nd. or 3rd. on the exhibits. On no account must a judge ever know whose stuff is whose, that's why the exhibits are numbered. So, now to start on the cakes. First you sort out those that are 'not according to the schedule' and write this on their cards. Then you cut them all in half and look at the way the fruit is dispersed and pick out the best ones. From these you look to see if the bottoms have the marks of the wire tray on them. If they have, that's a mark against them, as this can be avoided by putting the cake onto a cloth before being placed on the tray. Then it is time to use the knife and tea cloth that you always carry with you. You just cut a little sliver to test the flavour, and as you cut you can tell if the cake is too crumbly or too sticky. You look too for an even texture; you can tell, for example, if the sugar has not been beaten well in because it will emerge as white spots on the top.

HINTS FOR COOKERY EXHIBITS

Jam Tartlets (Short crust pastry)

Pastry should be about one-sixth of an inch thick and tartlets should not be too deep. The texture of the pastry should be crisp and 'short' in the mouth, not hard or brittle, and the colour should be a light golden brown. The jam should be a smooth layer, and all the tartlets should be a uniform shape, colour and size.

Jam Tart on a Plate

As above, but the edge may be decorated to give the double thickness, e.g. tiny cut-out pastry shapes, scalloped or fluted. The edge should not be too wide in relation to the size of the tart. A thin lattice of pastry may be arranged over the jam, but most important, the bottom pastry should be quite cooked and crisp under the jam filling.

Madeira Cake

This cake should be a pale golden brown. The top should be slightly domed and almost free from cracks. The sides should be straight with a thin golden crust on both sides and top. The texture should be even and fairly fine, not close or tight, and there should be no disfiguring cake rack marks on the bottom. The flavour is, of course, very important. Sometimes lemon is used, sometimes vanilla.

Plain Fruit Cake

A domed but not pointed top is desirable, some slight cracking is permissible but there should not be any burnt fruit on the surface. Inside the cake the fruit should be evenly distributed. Other points as for Madeira Cake.

68

Rich Fruit Cake (more than half fat to flour with corresponding amount of sugar and eggs)

The top should be flat, or almost so. Fruit on the outside should not be hard or burnt. The fruit inside should be evenly distributed. The colour of the crust and crumb should be a rich dark brown, the crust should be thin and the texture fine and moist, not heavy, close or soggy. The cake should cut cleanly and not crumble.

Plain Scones

The size, shape and colour should be uniform. They should have a smooth finish and be unglazed. 2" - 2 1/2" is a good size for round scones. They should be a pale golden brown and have a firm but springy texture when pressed between fingers. The flavour can usually be improved by a pinch of salt. They should not have sugar or fruit in, otherwise they really belong to 'Sweet Scones' or Fruit Scones and should then have glazed tops.

Sponge Sandwich (Fatless Sponge)

A plain flour will give a closer texture to a sponge than self-raising flour, but a more open texture is still acceptable.

The colour should be pale golden brown. The thickness of each layer should be uniform and the tops should be level. It is best to bake in two tins otherwise the jam soaks in too much on cut surfaces. Too much jam should not be used, and the cakes should be sandwiched with insides together.

Sponge Cakes

As for Sponge Sandwich, and the outside crust should show evidence of correct coating of tin (flour and sugar dusting over the oiled tin).

Gingerbread

This should be glossy and evenly baked with a reasonably flat top, no peaks or cracks. The whole slab should be shown unless the schedule states 'pieces'. A slab is usually about 10" x 6". It really should taste of ginger. Sometimes fruit and/or nuts are included in the recipe.

Shortbread

This should look smooth, neat, be evenly shaped and be of uniform colour. It should have a bright appearance, not look muddy, or be overcooked at the edges. It is important that it is 'short' right through and that it has a good flavouring.

Fancy Biscuits

These should be more or less the same size, though not necessarily the same shape. Each one can be decorated differently. Tasteful colouring of the icing is important, and Royal icing is better than water icing.

Biscuits (A plate of six biscuits undecorated)

These should be small, not too thick and baked through so that they are crisp. Size, colour and shape should be even.

Small Fancy Cakes

All must have a cake base. Assorted designs show more skill than a number all alike. A variety of decorating mediums may be used, e.g. cream, almond paste, icing, butter icing, etc. also nuts, fruits like cherries and angelica may be used in a design.

The cakes should be uniform in size though not necessarily in shape. The quality of icing and butter cream is important, but flavourings should not be over emphasised, especially cocoa.

Small cakes may be shown in paper cases but they need not have been cooked in them.

There will no doubt be other items included on the schedule but most of the points dealt with here apply in one way or another.

Loaf of White Bread (Yeast Dough)

Note: A 1 lb. loaf means it should weigh 1 lb. after cooking. The shape and colour should be uniform and true to type. The underneath should be free from kneading cracks and be a warm golden brown colour. 'Oven spring' of tin loaves should be even. The bottom and edges of a loaf should be clean, and the crust should be smooth, a crisp golden brown with no ugly cracks. When cut, the crumb mixture should be light, fine and even, free from streakiness and holes. The flavour of the bread should be well developed and free of any suggestion of yeasty sourness.

The crumb texture of brown bread should be close, more moist and less springy to the touch than white bread.

Bread Rolls

These should be even in size though not necessarily the same shape. They should be well risen and have a neat shape and appearance. They must feel light in relation to their size. They must not show signs of ugly kneading marks. If an egg glaze is used this should be applied carefully.

FLOWER ARRANGING AND JUDGING

This is a lovely art, creating our own designs out of nature's beauty, and essentially it is something you do for sheer pleasure. However, many shows do have a class for flower arrangements, and as I both enter and act as a judge, I will pass on a few of the principles used in judging.

Interpretation of the Schedule

This needs very careful thought. For instance, if the class is for an 'Arrangement for Welcome', you would need to use nice bright flowers, yellows and reds, not mauves and grey, the dark colours, which attractive though the flowers may be, are not cheerful or warm.

Design

This is very important. A good design has a good pattern and balance. You need to make sure that the smaller flowers which are more graceful are at the top of the design and the larger are lower down the scale.

Scale

This means that the flowers in the arrangement must be in scale with the vase or container. Many really beautiful arrangements have been spoilt by the vase being too big or too small, or even the wrong shape for the arrangement.

Balance

If you were to draw an imaginary line through the centre of the arrangement, each side should appear a visually equal balance.

Colour

As you judge an arrangement you have to decide for yourself if the colour in the flower or plant material used in the design fully interprets what is asked for by the schedule.

Suitability of Container

Both in colour, texture and harmony the container should suit the material it holds. A base is considered part of the container providing it holds a water retaining receptacle about it. This could be a small tin or dish (I have used old polish tins and even an old sugar basin) but once it has been hidden it will be the base which is in colour, texture or size with the flowers used. If your design is meant to suggest something of a bygone age then you would try to use a period piece as a container, while a modern design demands large spaces and contrasts.

Condition of Plant Material

There is nothing more likely to spoil an arrangement than 'Droopy' foliage. The hints I have earlier about picking in good time and making sure your flowers have a good drink apply here.

Distinction and Originality

When you are judging an arrangement this is the most difficult part to define. I look for some original thought, which might include the use of drapes - a piece of cloth behind an arrangement helps to give it colour and height - or the unusual placement of different sized bases.

One final word, do make sure that if you have wired any of your plant material, the wire does not show. These are tips for shows, but the important thing to remember is that God gave us flowers to enjoy whether they are growing in the garden or beautifully arranged in a vase - and what mother hasn't been moved by the present of a bunch of Buttercups crammed into a jam-jar or made into a picture at school and lovingly brought home for Mothering Sunday? I often make flower pictures to give as presents or for a sale at fund-raising bazaars.

WINE MAKING

One of the nicest things about a garden is that as well as putting things back into the soil to give it strength, you can take things out of the garden and put them into yourself to do the same thing! I make around 80 gallons of wine from the produce of the garden and the surrounding area. My shed has been called an Aladdin's Cave of wine. Certainly the colours of the wine are beautiful when the light comes in through the window into the semi-darkness and all the golds and reds and orange shades shine against the wooden walls. I sometimes think it is a shame that commercially produced wine is only made from grapes. Of course there are all sorts of consistencies and tastes to be had from the grape, but when you think of all the other produce you can use, then the varieties are endless, and I think, more fun. You can, in fact make wine out of anything organic, even onions and lettuce, though I have to confess that I have never tried these two.

Among my favourites are parsnip, wheat and loganberry. I must warn you, if you haven't tried it, that home-made wine is very strong and powerful. Many's the time we have had friends call in for an evening and out has come a bottle of our home-made, and it's fine until you get outside in the air, and then you wonder what has hit you!

You will be able to get detailed instructions for wine making elsewhere, but I want to just give you a few tips to put you on the right track and whet (or should it be wet?) your appetite.

The actual processes of making the wine vary slightly in each recipe. Some say pour boiling water on to the fruit, others say boil the fruit and water together. If you are using oranges, lemons, or grapefruit is is essential that on no account should any of the white pith under the rind get into the wine as this will produce a harsh, bitter taste and perhaps an undrinkable wine. It is also important that your wine is covered at all times to exclude any stray bacteria. Once you have started your wine keep the fermentation jars or demijohns where a temperature of

74

65 F will be maintained. Fermentation should continue uninterrupted until all the sugar and nutrients have been used and the alcohol content of the wine is sufficient to inhibit the further growth of the yeast. Should fermentation slow down or cease too soon and the bubbles of gas no longer appear through the fermentation lock, check the following:-

1. That the temperature is correct. Fermentation will cease if the temperature is too high or too low.

2. That there is neither too much or too little sugar.

3. If the wine has been fortified, make sure that there is not too much alcohol.

4. That there is not too much acid.

5. That you have not used too much yeast starter.

When fermentation finishes the wine will clear from the top downwards and a thick deposit will form at the bottom of the demijohn. Now siphon off the wine into a clean jar and top it up. If you have no wine left to do this, use a little sugar dissolved in boiling water. Cork the jar securely and leave for a couple of months before racking off again to leave any further sediment. Again, top up and recork the jar. Finally bottle off when you are ready. Incidentally, dark bottles are best for keeping the colour of a dark wine, but I prefer to use clear demijohns so that I can see exactly where the sediment is.

RECIPES

I make a Yeast Starter which I use for all the following recipes. Put 1/2 pint of warm water into a bottle with 11/2 teaspoons of wine yeast and mix. After about half an hour the mixture begins to froth, it is then poured into the container which holds the fruit or vegetable mixture. Sprinkle a teaspoon of nutrient on top and add two Campden tablets. Give the lot a stir. There are other methods, but this is the one I use. Of course, it goes without saying, that all the utensils, bottles etc., that you use are kept scrupulously clean.

Parsnip Wine

4 lbs. parsnips
3 lb. sugar
1 gallon water
1/2 lb. raisins
Rind and juice of 2 lemons and 2 oranges
Yeast

Scrub and then slice the parsnips, removing any bad parts. Add the thinly peeled rinds of the fruit and boil until the parsnips are just tender. Strain, then add the rest of the water, stir in the sugar, chopped raisins, the juice from the citrus fruits and yeast. Pour into fermentation jars and add a little sugar during fermentation until it stops working, then rack, mature and bottle.

Parsley Wine

1 lb. parsley
2 lemons
3 lbs. sugar
Lump of ginger
Yeast
1 gallon water

Boil the parsley in water until tender, then strain into large container. Add sugar, thinly peeled rind of lemons and the ginger. Stir well. When lukewarm add yeast and leave covered for two weeks. Strain into fermentation jars and leave until fermentation ceases, then rack, mature and bottle.

Sloe Wine (very good)

3 lbs. ripe sloes
1 gallon water
2¹/₂ lbs. sugar
Yeast
Campden tablet
Pectic-enzyme

   Clean and stalk the sloes and then pour the boiling water over them. When cool mash them and add I campden tablet and one teaspoonful of pectic-enzyme. Leave covered for 4 days, then strain. Stir in sugar and yeast. Pour into fermentation jars leave until fermentation ceases, then rack mature, and bottle.

Dandelion Wine

1 gallon dandelion flowers (measure in a gallon bucket)
1 orange and 1 lemon
3 lbs. sugar
1 gallon water
Yeast

The dandelions must be picked in the sunshine when the flowers are fully open. Use only the yellow parts. Put blooms in cold water and bring to the boil, then simmer for 10 minutes. Strain on to the sugar and add the thinly peeled rinds of the orange and lemon. Stir. When lukewarm add the juice of the citrus fruits and the yeast. Cover and leave in a warm place. After two days pour into a fermentation jar. When fermentation is completed, rack, mature and bottle.

Oak Leaf Wine

1 gallon young oak leaves
1 gallon boiling water
2 oranges and 1 lemon
3 lbs. sugar
Yeast

Pour the boiling water over the oak leaves and leave to stand, well covered for 24 hours. Strain and boil with the sugar and the thin rind and juice of the oranges and lemon for 20 minutes. When cool strain again. Add the yeast and pour into fermentation jars and leave until fermentation ceases. Rack, mature and bottle.
Note: The flavour of this wine can be varied by picking the leaves at various times throughout the season, from when they are very young through to when they begin to turn brown. A similar wine can be made with walnut leaves.

Sloe Gin

Prick with a pin 1 lb. of dry sloes then put into a 1/2 gallon jar with 1 oz. sweet almonds and 6 oz. white sugar. Pour on 1 bottle of gin and cover. Shake the jar daily for three months. Strain, bottle and seal. This improves with keeping.

Carrot Wine

4 lbs. well scrubbed carrots
2 1/2 lbs. sugar (mix brown & white)
1 lb. raisins
2 lemons, 2 oranges
Yeast

Boil the carrots until they are soft, then strain the liquid and add the sugar to it. Stir well and simmer with the thinly peeled rinds of the oranges and lemons for a further 20 minutes. Make the liquid up to a gallon. When cool add the juice of the citrus fruits. Add the yeast, leave covered for five days. Strain into fermentation jars and leave in a warm place until it stops working. Rack, mature and bottle in the usual way.

Note: The longer this one is kept, the better!

Gorse Wine

This is a nice wine, especially when it is mixed, gallon for gallon with gooseberry. I pick the flowers from the nearby common.

1/2 gallon of gorse flowers
1 gallon water
2 1/2 - 3 lbs. Demerara sugar
1 orange and 1 lemon
Yeast

Put the flowers in a net bag and simmer for fifteen minutes. Stir in the sugar until dissolved, then put into a big container. Slice the orange and lemon and add to the cooling liquid. When lukewarm add the yeast. Cover and leave for a week. Strain into fermentation jar, and when fermentation stops, rack and bottle.

Elderberry Wine

Cheap one this, from the hedgerows.

6 pints water
3 lbs. of elderberries
3 lbs. sugar
Yeast

Boil the elderberries in the water and then crush. When lukewarm add half the sugar which has previously been made into a syrup. Add the yeast. Cover well. Allow to ferment for four days, then strain into fermentation jars. After six days, top up with the rest of the sugar as a syrup. Ferment to a finish, rack, mature and bottle.

Blackberry Wine

6 lbs. blackberries
1 gallon water
3 lbs. sugar
1 lemon
Yeast

Wash blackberries, peel the lemon thinly and put them all into a large container. Pour over 1 gallon of water and let this stand for three days, stirring daily. Strain on to the sugar and stir well. Add the juice of the lemon. Put in the yeast. Leave in a warm place for 24 hours, pour into fermentation jars. When fermentation has ceased, rack and bottle.

Apple Wine

12 - 14 lbs. mixed apples
1 gallon water
$2^{1/2}$ lbs. sugar
Campden tablet
Pectic-enzyme
Yeast

Crush the cleaned apples and add them to 1 gallon of cold water in which one Campden tablet has been dissolved. Sprinkle on 1 teaspoonful of pectic-enzyme. Leave covered to soak for 3 days, then strain and squeeze. Add sugar, then put into fermentation jars. When fermentation ceases, rack, mature and bottle.
Note: 1 lb. of raisins added to this will give more body.

Red Clover Wine

1 gallon clover blossoms
2 lemons & 2 oranges
1 gallon water
3 lbs. sugar
Yeast

Boil sugar and water, simmer for five minutes, then cool. Place the lemon and orange peel in a large container with the flower heads. Pour over the cool liquid and stir. Add the yeast. Leave covered for seven days, stirring daily. Strain into fermentation jars. Keep in a warm place. Finally rack and bottle.

Mayflower or Hawthorn Blossom Wine

1/2 gallon mayflowers
3 lbs. sugar
1/2 lb. raisins
1 gallon water
Yeast
1 lb. wheat

Put the flowers into a container. Boil the sugar and water together, then pour over the blossoms. Chop the raisins and add them to the must when it is lukewarm, together with the wheat and yeast. Leave to ferment for 10 days, well covered, then strain into fermentation bottles. Ferment to a finish, rack, mature and bottle.

Rice Wine

3 lbs. rice
1 lb. raisins
3 lbs. sugar
1 gallon water
1 pinch of isinglass
Yeast

Put the rice and sugar into a large container and cover with warm water. Add chopped raisins and yeast. Sprinkle over the isinglass. Leave covered for nine days before straining into fermentation jars. Rack and bottle.
Note: Try to keep this as long as possible as it tends to be a little harsh at first.

Poor Man's Brandy - Potato and Wheat

2 lbs. potatoes
2 lbs. chopped raisins
1 gallon water
1 lb. crushed wheat
3 lbs. Demerara sugar
Rind and juice of 2 lemons and 1 orange
Yeast

Scrub and cut the potatoes into small pieces and put into a large container with the crushed wheat, the raisins and the peel of the citrus fruit. Pour on one gallon of boiling water and leave covered for 3 days. Strain and squeeze. Stir in the sugar, fruit juice and yeast. Put into fermentation jars and leave until finished. Rack, mature and bottle.
Note: Do try to leave this for at least two years.
Incidentally, don't throw the raisins away when you strain off the wine, or feed them to the birds! I use mine in a fruit cake.

Cowslip or Oxslip Wine

1 gallon cowslips (just the yellow parts)
1 gallon water
2 oranges & 2 lemons
3 lbs. sugar
Yeast

Boil the sugar in the water for 5 minutes, then cool. Peel the oranges and lemons thinly and put into a large container with the juice of the fruit and the cowslip heads. Pour the liquid over and stir. Add yeast and leave covered for 5 days. Stir daily. Strain and place in fermentation jars. Leave until ready to rack, mature and bottle.
Please remember that it is illegal to pick wild flowers, so if you want to use this old recipe, make sure you use cultivated flowers from the garden.

Wheat Wine

2 pints wheat
3 lbs. Demerara sugar
1 gallon water
2 lemons
2 lbs. raisins
Yeast

Put the chopped raisins, sugar and wheat with the thinly peeled rind and the juice of the lemon in the water. Add the yeast, cover and leave for 10 days, stirring daily. Strain when all fermentation ceases, rack, mature and bottle.
This is another one that is best if kept for two years.

Pea Pod Wine

4 lbs. pea pods
3 lbs. sugar
1 lemon
1 gallon water
Yeast

Boil the pea pods with the lemon peel until tender. Strain on to the sugar and stir. When lukewarm add the juice of the lemon and yeast. Stir and leave covered in a warm place for twenty-four hours. Pour into fermentation jars. When fermentation ceases, rack, mature and bottle.

Blackcurrant Wine

3 lbs. blackcurrants
1 gallon water
Wine Yeast
Pectic-enzyme
3 lbs. sugar

Crush the blackcurrants and pour 4 pints of boiling water over them. Mash well. When lukewarm add pectic-enzyme and half the sugar as syrup, and the yeast as directed. Cover well and allow to ferment in pulp for four days. Strain well and put into fermentation jars. Add the rest of the sugar as syrup, topping up to 1 gallon after another six days. Allow to ferment to a finish, rack and bottle.

JUDGING HOME-MADE WINES

At many of the horticultural and agricultural shows there is a wine section. Hundreds of bottles with all shades of wine to fill a big table with the various sections.

A very small money prize, say 50p or so, may be awarded, or perhaps a certificate. Nonetheless, the competition is keen. There are rules for the competition, but a good deal depends on the personal taste of the judge. Here's how to judge home-made wine and a few hints on how to exhibit it.

1. Make sure you read the schedule.

2. Make sure that you have all the equipment you will need judging -
   corkscrew, glasses for tasting, a spittoon (pail), bowl for washing glasses, glass cloth, dry biscuits or bread, pen or pencil, a marking sheet and a show schedule.

3. Standard to look for:-
   (a) presentation, (b) clarity, (c) colour,
   (d) aroma and bouquet, (e) flavour, balance and quality.

When exhibiting:

1. Make sure that the wine is in the right class.

2. Make sure that it is presented in the correct type of bottle. For show purposes the bottle should be of clear glass.

3. The bottle should be filled so that when the cork is pushed right home the air space in the neck of the bottle is about 3/4" from the bottom.
   of the cork.

4. Only corks with flanged heads should be used.

5. The label should be according to type or ingredient. A stick on label should be 2" x 3/4" and fixed above the bottom edge.

THE BUSY YEAR

- January -

You might think it strange, but for me, this is the month for preserving, changing some of the things you've gathered from the garden into more lasting forms - although where food is concerned, nothing seems to last longer than the time it takes to cook and eat it! Seriously though, I don't think that nowadays enough attention is given to the art of pickling. What with freezers being able to keep things fresh, people have forgotten how to pickle and preserve, and we are in danger of losing all the beautiful and delicate tastes and textures which only the pickling process can bring out.

This is my favourite recipe for pickling meat:-

About 3 lbs. of meat
1 lb. of black treacle
1$^1/_2$ lbs. cooking salt
1 oz. saltpetre
1 lb. brown sugar
2 pints of stout or ale

Method

Put the treacle, sugar and ale in a saucepan and boil for five minutes. Rub the ham or other joint all over with the salts. Place the ham in a suitable container and then pour the hot mixture over it. The meat should be left in this pickling mixture for four weeks and turned each day so that the liquor soaks well in. At the end of four weeks, remove the ham and hang it inside an old pillow case until required (You really need an old fashioned larder for this, but the garage will do.) Remember to soak the ham in cold water 24 hours before you wish to cook it.

Pork is a wonderful meat, there is so much you can do with it, and so little waste. I try to buy a half side of pork which I can cut up how I want. Here's another recipe which uses pickling, and some of the parts of the pig that those who don't know any better, might throw away.

Brawn or Suffolk Pork Cheese

1/2 pig's head
1 trotter
1 small onion
1 small carrot
2 cloves of garlic
2 bay leaves
2 sprigs parsley
2 sprigs thyme
8 peppercorns
2 tablespoons wine vinegar
Water to cover
1/2 bottle white whine (I use home-made apple wine)
Lemon juice to taste
Salt and pepper to taste
Method

Put all the ingredients in a large pan (except the lemon juice and the wine) and cook together until the meat falls off the bone. The slower the meat cooks, the better. This is where that old paraffin stove of mine comes into its own. When the meat is cold take it off the bone and cut up very small. Strain the liquid off, reserving about a pint of it. Return the meat, the strained stock, the wine and the lemon juice to the preserving pan and boil up for about 1/2 hour. Turn into basins or moulds and leave to set.

Rendering down lard

I often have a little laugh to myself about the way fashions change. Whoever would have thought when I was a girl, that a kitchen treat would end up being sold in packets at some great price. But that is exactly what has happened to those lovely scrunchy bits left at the end of rendering down pork fat to make lard.

At the end of a baking session when the oven is still warm, take a large meat pan and place into it all the pieces of fat you have cut off your joints of pork. The pieces should not be too large. As the pieces shrink pour off into a basin all the hot liquid which will, when cold turn into beautiful lard. This is lovely for making pastry, and as I've said, at the end of it all, you are left with some good pork scratchings, which only need a bit of salt and a sprinkle of vinegar to make a treat for the children.

Marmalade

This recipe was given me by two old ladies, sisters, who were living in the village when I first married. They used to make a lot of jam and marmalade for the church fetes.

2 lbs. Seville oranges
4 pints water
2 lemons
4 lbs. sugar

Method

Wash and shred the fruit. Put the pips into a muslin bag and put with the fruit and water into a basin and leave overnight. Next day, place in the preserving pan and bring to the boil slowly, and then simmer till the peel is soft. The contents of the pan will reduce by half. Remove the bag of pips. Add the sugar, stir until dissolved, then boil quickly until a set is achieved. Cool a little before putting into warmed jars. This will stop the peel from rising to the top.

Lemon Curd

2 oz. margarine
1 lb. sugar
4 lemons
4 eggs

Method

Put the grated rind of the lemons, the juice, margarine and sugar into either a double saucepan or a basin over hot water. While this is getting hot beat the eggs. Stir into other ingredients and cook until thick. This curd keeps very well.

January is often the month when your purse is almost empty, so I thought this might be the place to put in a few recipes for when times are hard.

End of Week Pudding

4 ozs. self-raising flour
4 ozs. breadcrumbs
4 ozs. suet
1 egg
Milk to mix
Salt to taste
Mixed herbs, chives or onions
Left over cooked meat or bacon

Method

Mix together flour, breadcrumbs, suet, egg and enough milk to make a stiff dough. Season with salt to taste, add herbs, chives or onions. Add the cooked meat, bacon or whatever you have to hand. Steam for 3 hours.
If you don't have any breadcrumbs, use flour instead but the pudding will not be quite as light. If you haven't any meat, you

90

can always serve this up with a good gravy and plenty of fried onions.

Poor Man's Dumpling

This is a good old Suffolk recipe. It was given to my mother by the wife of an old gardener from Needham Market.

1 medium cabbage
8 good rashers of bacon (not too thinly cut)
8 dumplings
Salt and pepper

Method

Cut the cabbage finely after washing it well. Place in saucepan, cover with boiling water and cook until tender. Drain well. Meanwhile, fry the bacon; make and boil the dumplings. Dish up the cabbage on a hot dish, arrange the dumplings around and place the bacon on top of the dumplings. Add salt and pepper. Pour off dripping.

Sheet Lighting

A good filler for children this one. We often had it when I was a child.

Method

Spread stale bread with margarine (butter if you like) then with Golden Syrup and fry in margarine. We thought this was a tremendous treat.

Now, if by the end of the month, you feel you can afford to give yourself a treat, why not try a really lovely old recipe:-

Ipswich Almond Pudding (circa 1741)

1¹/2 ozs. breadcrumbs
3/4 pint double cream
1/4 lb. ground almonds
A little rose or orange flower water
4 eggs
2 ozs. castor sugar

Method

Warm the cream and pour onto the breadcrumbs. Stir in the sugar, almonds and flavouring. Beat up the yolks and two whites of eggs. Mix well with the other ingredients and pour into a buttered pie dish. Dot a few pieces of butter over the top. Bake for about half an hour in a slow oven.

- February -

This is mostly a cleaning month for me, a time for getting the whole place shipshape. I know a lot of people would say that this is the wrong time, but I like to get the decorating underway in February, with the help of a kind friend. It's rather cosy to be making the house look bright and fresh when its so cold and dark outside. And after a hard day's painting or paper-hanging, what better way to relax in the evening than with a glass of my home-made mead! Mind you, you have to make it first, and this is a good month to do that.

Old English Mead

It is said that this was drunk in the Stone Age. I don't know about that, but certainly our ancestors are reputed to have drunk mead from horns when they feasted in their huts during the long, cold winter. We don't use horns and a meagre glassful is usually enough to make the cold outside seem a long way away. My recipe uses melted snow, but don't worry if you live in one of those areas where the snow has more chemicals in it than the petrol tank of your car, because tap water is fine, as long as it is on the soft side. They say that mead is awfully good for you and does wonders for the complexion. As to that, all I can say is that it was known to give Ernie a slight reddening of the nose!

Method

Take three pounds of pure honey, not this commercialised stuff, but the real thing from a beekeeper, minus, of course, the wax cone. Then you need a gallon of soft water, preferably from melted snow. Boil the water, then tip the honey into a bucket and pour on the boiling water. Stir thoroughly, then while still warm add one teaspoonful of wine yeast and nutrient and let it work. This is a very simple recipe which almost makes itself.

Talking of simple things, this seems to be a good spot to say a few words about my winter recipes. It seems to me that what with all these slimming crazes, packaged meals and frozen foods, the seasons are being taken out of eating. Now, I don't know about you, but for me, that's one of the joys of eating, realising the time of the year and appreciating the taste of the first of the crop, whether it be that lovely mouth-watering freshness of a young green pea or the crunchiness of the sprouts after the first frost of the autumn. You know, when you're stirring a pot of good hot winter food, like beef stew and dumplings, or when you're coming home in the cold to a good solid winter meal, it almost makes you glad to be struggling through the bad weather, because the food at the end is like a big reward. I'd like to see the old traditions of seasonal cooking coming back, I can tell you, though I do believe that of recent years, chefs in hotels and restaurants have begun to realise that there are other vegetables than frozen peas and beans, and that swedes and parsnips, properly cooked, can be just right for winter dishes.

Beef Stew With Dumplings

1¹/₄lbs. stewing beef
Teaspoon mustard (dry)
1 pint water
2 onions
2 large carrots
Tablespoon flour
Chopped parsley (if liked)
Seasoning
Little dripping or fat
2 Oxo cubes or similar

Method

Chop beef and roll in flour with seasoning and mustard. Melt dripping or fat in frying pan and fry meat until brown all over. Place in saucepan with chopped onions, carrots and parsley and Oxo cubes dissolved in water. Bring to the boil then lower heat and simmer for 1¹/₂ hours. Add up to ¹/₂ pint water if necessary.

Dumplings

¹/₂ lb. self-raising flour
¹/₂ teaspoon salt
Enough water to bind

Method

Put flour and salt into a bowl, mix with water and form into small balls. Place in stew about fifteen minutes before you are ready to serve it.

Pork and Onion Pudding

The pudding:
12 ozs. self-raising flour
6 ozs. suet
$1/2$ teaspoon salt
Enough water to bind

The filling:
$1 1/2$ lbs. pork pieces
1 lb. onions
Pepper and salt
Water to cover

Method

Mix the dry ingredients for the crust together with the water. Roll out the dough and then line a ready greased pudding basin. Reserve some of the dough for the lid of the pudding. Cut the pork and onions into small pieces and arrange them in layers inside the crust. Season each layer. Cover with a little water. Fit pastry lid on the top and then cover with greased paper and finally a pudding cloth. The pudding should be steamed for four to five hours.

The recipe for beef stew and dumplings was one of my mum's standbys. We used to have it on Wednesday as the butcher used to call on Tuesdays and Thursdays. We tended to have the cheaper cuts of meat when I was young, not only because they were cheaper, but with rationing both during and after the War, joints just did not go far enough for a family. Of course, living in the country we were luckier than the townsfolk, we could at least get plenty of rabbits. There was a story that went the rounds in the village during the War about the evacuee who was told he ought to have a dose of something to keep him regular. "Don't know about that," the youngster replied, "I reckon I need a ferret!"

Those boys and girls who found themselves set down in the

middle of Suffolk at the beginning of the War must have found our ways strange, especially some of the foods they had to eat. I don't suppose that many of their mothers made stock from bones and vegetables. You can't beat the stock you get from a marrow bone, that's the lovely thick, knobbly one from a cow's leg. You get it from the butcher and if you ask nicely, he'll chop it for you, then you boil it and boil it and then leave it for a day. The resulting liquid turns into a luscious thick jelly which is the basis of your soup. All you need do is skim off any fat and then add any flavouring that takes your fancy. Incidentally, don't throw the fat away, you can use that in pastry or whatever happens to need some lard.

To round off, how about a couple of sweet recipes.

Treacle Custard

This is an old recipe from Southwold.

Short crust pastry
1 egg
2 tablespoons Golden Syrup

Method

Line a plate with short crust pastry.
Beat up the egg, warm the syrup. Beat the two together, then pour into the pastry lined plate.
Bake in a slow oven until golden brown. Eat cold when set.

Brotherly Love

When making bread leave aside 1 lb. of dough. Roll it out to 1/2" thick. Scatter over this 2 ozs. sugar and 1 oz. lard broken into small pieces. Roll up like a Swiss Roll and cut into slices. Bake for about 1/2 hour in a hot oven.

- March -

This is a very busy month for me, taken up with getting things ready in the garden. I also seem to do a lot of talking this month to Women's Institutes, Townswomen's Guilds and Church Groups in the surrounding villages, so I want meals that are not only easily prepared and don't mind waiting if I'm a bit on the late side, so it's still casserole time, especially liver and bacon casserole, but I also want things I can eat quickly, so I make up a batch of liver paste (that's exactly the same as the posh French named variety) to have on toast as a snack.

Liver Paste

4 ozs. lamb's or chicken's liver
2 rashers streaky bacon
1 tablespoon tomato puree
Few drops Worcester Sauce
1 oz. flour
1 oz. margarine
1/4 pint stock or 1/4 pint Oxo or similar beef extract
Pinch herbs
Salt and pepper

Method

Lightly fry the chopped liver and bacon; when cool pound up or mince finely. Make a sauce with the flour, fat and stock. Mix together the meat and the sauce, add the other ingredients. Place the mixture in a casserole or small loaf tin; cover with foil. Put the tin into a large container half filled with water. Bake in this water bath for about 1 hour at 350 F.

Mince and Cheese Crumble

1 lb. mince
1 oz. dripping
2 sliced onions
2 tablespoons tomato puree
6 tomatoes or carrots
1/2 pint stock
salt and pepper

Topping:

4 ozs. flour
2 ozs. margarine
3 ozs. grated cheese

Method

Fry the onion in hot fat, then add the meat, stirring with a fork until it is all lightly browned. Add seasoning. Mix in the stock and pour into a suitable sized dish. Place sliced tomatoes or carrots on top of the meat. To make topping, rub the fat into the flour, add cheese and season well. Sprinkle the crumble topping over the meat mixture.
Bake for 35 - 45 minutes at 375 F.

Country Apple Cake

1 lb. cooking apples
1 oz. butter
2 tablespoons lemon juice
6 ozs. raisins
2 ozs. shelled walnuts
6 ozs. currants
6 ozs. margarine
10 ozs. plain flour

1¹/₂ teaspoonful bicarbonate of soda
2 tablespoonsful Golden Syrup
1 teaspoon ground cinnamon
2 eggs
pinch of salt

Method

Peel, core and chip the apples. Cook with the lemon juice and butter over a low heat until quite soft. Beat to a puree and leave until cold.
Line an 8" diameter cake tin with double thickness greaseproof paper. Mix the flour, salt, bicarb. and spices. Sift twice. Chop the walnuts and add to the dried fruit.
Cream the fat and syrup, then add the eggs. Stir in the flour mixture, alternating with the apple puree. Add the fruit and nuts. Turn into the tin and make a deep hollow in the centre.
Bake on the middle shelf of a pre-heated oven at 325 F for at least 1¹/₂ - 2 hours, or until quite firm and brown.
Leave the cake to cool for half an hour before turning out, and leave until quite cold before removing the paper.
Store for a week before cutting.

- April -

"When you hear the cuckoo shout, 'tis time to plant your tatties out". Traditionally, Good Friday was the day when the gardeners started their work, and certainly, April is the month when the life of the village and my garden both seem to spring into bloom. My grandfather always tried to get his potatoes put in on Good Friday - I suppose this went back to the fact that it was the farm worker's day off, so he got a chance to do a bit in his own garden during daylight hours. There's another saying about planting on Good Friday and that's to do with parsley, that it is best if sown on that day. I don't know why parsley should inspire quite so many old sayings and superstitions, but have you noticed how many of them are to do with women?

"Parsley should only be sown by a woman, so that she will flourish like the parsley." Then there's the one about where parsley does well, the woman rules the household!

Not that the men could do without their womenfolk, especially when they used to rely on them to bring them something tasty to eat while they were working in the fields. In Suffolk you would often see a workman sit down at the side of the field with his flask and something like my mum's 'Stickies' or the good old Suffolk rusk. The following recipe was my Aunt Liz's. Some people use one egg, I put two in because it gives a nice rich taste. You can vary the recipe and add cheese if you fancy.

Suffolk Rusks

1 lb. self-raising flour
Good pinch of salt
6 ozs. fat (3 ozs. lard, 3 ozs. margarine)
2 eggs and a little water to mix

Method

Rub the fats into the flour and salt, then with the beaten eggs mix to a smooth dough. Roll out to 1 inch thickness and cut into rounds - about 2 1/2" - and bake at 450 F for about 10 - 12 minutes. Remove from the oven, and cut open, then return to the oven for a further 10 - 15 minutes or until a nice golden brown. When cold these rusks are delicious served with a bit of butter or cheese. .

Of course, April is often Eastertide, so we must have some traditional Easter recipes.

Hot Cross Buns

1 lb. strong flour
1 teaspoon salt
2 ozs. butter

1 egg
1/2 pint milk
1 oz. fresh yeast or 1/2 oz. dried yeast
1 oz. sugar
1 1/2 ozs. chopped peel
2 ozs. sultanas
1 teaspoon mixed spice

Method

Add the yeast and sugar to the warm milk and leave for five minutes to become frothy. Add the melted butter and egg. Warm and sieve the flour and salt. Put yeast mixture into mixing bowl and add warmed dried ingredients, plus fruit and spices, to make a soft dough. Beat well until the mixture leaves the sides of the bowl. If you have used your hand to beat the mixture instead of a spoon, then the mixture should leave the hand cleanly. Leave it to prove in a warm place covered with a cloth. When doubled in size, knead and shape into buns. Leave to prove for 15 - 20 minutes covered with a greased polythene bag to prevent skin forming. When ready for the oven place a small cross of pastry on each bun and brush the top with a little milk and sugar glaze. Bake at 400 F for about 15 - 20 minutes.

The traditional cake for Easter is the Simnel Cake. It gets its name from the Latin word similia which means the best quality flour. The cake was originally baked for servant girls to take home with them to give to their mothers when they were allowed home for a day off on what has become known as Mothering Sunday. The eleven balls of marzipan on the top of the cake are supposed to represent the apostles, Judas being excluded. The finished cake is browned lightly under the grill to give the marzipan a toasty colour.

Simnel Cake

6 ozs. soft margarine
6 ozs. soft brown sugar
3 large eggs
6 ozs. plain flour
3 level teaspoons mixed spice
1 level teaspoon baking powder
1 level tablespoon marmalade
10 ozs. mixed dried fruit
2 ozs. glacé cherries
1/2 lb. marzipan

Method

Cream the margarine and sugar, beating well with a wooden spoon. Add the beaten eggs, then fold in the sieved flour with the spices and baking powder. Finally stir in the fruit and cherries. Grease and line with greaseproof paper a 7" cake tin. Put half the mixture into the tin smoothing it flat. Roll out some marzipan on a board lightly dusted with castor sugar and cut out a 7" round. Place this on the mixture in the tin. Fill the tin with the remaining cake mixture, smooth the top and make a hollow in the centre. Bake for 2 1/2 hours at 300 F. When the cake has cooled, brush the top with the marmalade. Roll out another circle of marzipan to fit the top of the cake, pinching the edges to form a decoration. With the left-over marzipan shape 11 small equal size balls and place these around the cake.

-May-

"When the Dogwood flower appear, frost will not again be here." What a lovely month May is, and a very busy one for me in the garden where I am planting out all the bedding plants, and gathering the flowers to make flower wines. Particularly useful at a time like this is a cake which will keep well, so that if I haven't had time to bake, I know that this old stand-by will help me out if I get unexpected visitors.

Matrimonial Cake

This gets its name from the fact that it has a rough crunchy top and a smooth filling with a firm base - just like a marriage, you have to take the rough with the smooth.

4 ozs. porridge oats
3 ozs. whole wheat flour
2 ozs. brown sugar
3 ozs. butter
Fillings:
8 ozs. dates
1 oz. brown sugar
4 fluid ozs. water

Method

Start with the filling. Chop the dates and cook gently with the sugar and water until soft, but not too sloppy. Leave to cool.
Mix the oats, flour and sugar. Rub in the butter until the mixture resembles crumbs. Put half this mixture into a greased tin about 7" square. Pat down firmly.
Spread with the date filling. Cover with the rest of the crumble mixture and pat down gently. Bake for 15 - 20 minutes just above the middle of the oven at 350 F until golden brown.
Cut into squares while still hot, but leave in the tin to cool.

*

At this time of year, it is lovely to have a nice joint of lamb for Sunday lunch, and when you think of lamb, then of course, mint sauce springs to mind. Well, here is something just a little bit different.

Spring Mint Preserve

1¹/₂ lbs. gooseberries or 2 lbs. apples
One-third pint cider vinegar
1 lb. sugar
2 large bunches mint

Method

Top and tail gooseberries. Cook them gently in vinegar with a bunch of mint until tender. Don't overcook. Discard the mint. Add the sugar and stir until dissolved. Cook until thick, stirring constantly. Add the chopped mint from the second bunch. Mix well and then put into small jars.

- June-

This is the month of the Church Fete and barbecues, so we are busy planning stalls and going round the village asking for gifts and arranging for people to help. And through all this, you can bet I am cooking as well, because what ever else, we do have to eat, even if there are times when we feel too busy to stop, or too tired for anything other than a snack. Now, as far as I am concerned, there are snacks, and snacks, and I'm talking about a good wholesome one, like this recipe of my mum's which is lovely to have with a good cup of tea on a warm June afternoon.

Mum's Stickies

1 lb. self-raising flour
8 ozs. lard
3 ozs. sugar
4 ozs. currants
Pinch of salt
1 egg

Method

Work the lard into the flour and salt until it resembles breadcrumbs. Beat the egg with a little water and mix to form a pastry. Roll out to the thickness of about half an inch. Spread the sugar and currants all over the pastry. Fold it over and roll out. Fold and roll again, then cut into squares and place on a flat tin or baking sheet. Bake in a hot oven for about 15 minutes.

Dad always had some of these put in his bag for his 'bait' when he worked in the fields.

Suffolk Haslett

This is another thing that was to be found in the men's lunch boxes in the old days. I like to eat it with a green salad.

1 lb. belly of pork
1 3/4 lbs. pigs liver
1 pigs heart
Salt and pepper to taste (about 1 teaspoonful of each)
1 heaped teaspoon fresh sage
1 egg
6 ozs. mixed brown and white breadcrumbs
4 tablespoonsful water
The veil from a pig's stomach or a cake tin

Method

Mince all the meats together. Mix in all the remaining ingredients until the mixture is on the dry side.

If using the pig's veil, stuff the mixture into it, otherwise pack it into a cake tin and cover with three or four rashers of streaky bacon. Place either the veil or the cake tin on a baking sheet and cook for a good thirty minutes at 350 F.

Rhubarb and Rose Petal Jam

Makes about 1³/4 lbs.

1 lb. trimmed rhubarb
1 lb. sugar
Juice of 1 lemon
4 handfuls of scented rose petals, red if possible

Method

Wipe the rhubarb, cut into small pieces and place in a bowl. Cover with the sugar, add the lemon juice and leave to stand overnight. Chop the rose petals and add to the rhubarb. Transfer all to a preserving pan. Bring to the boil, and boil until setting point is reached. Pour into warmed jars, cover and label.
Note: As an alternative to rose petals you can use 2 ozs. finely chopped angelica (fresh or crystallized) or 2 ozs. of ginger.

- JULY -

There are times during this month when I don't know which way to turn, and I mean that quite literally because sometimes we have more visitors to the garden than we know what to do with. In 1984 for example, we had 31 coach loads during July, and I can't tell you how many other people turned up by car, or cycle or even on foot. Without any doubt, this is my busiest month of the year, and I'm hither and thither at flower shows as well as everything else. Then of course, there is still all the soft fruit to be picked and dealt with. Now, as I've said earlier, there was a time when I thought that a deep freeze was not for the likes of me, but nowadays, I don't know what I would do without it, for at least it allows me to pick my fruit and then make it into whatever I want when I have the time. But, however much of a 'muck sweat' as we say in Suffolk, that

I'm in, I always make time to pickle some walnuts. These must be picked when they are still green in early July.

Pickled Walnuts

Test to see if the walnuts are ready by pushing a needle into the green shells. If it goes in easily, then they are just right for pickling.

Method

Prick the walnuts with a fork and leave them in brine for a week.
Drain and place them on old dishes that will not hurt if they are stained, and leave the nuts in the sunshine or bright light for two days. Turn them over once or twice until the nuts are black all over. Pack them into jars, cover with cold spiced vinegar, and seal the jars well.

*

I need to make cakes and biscuits that don't require too much time, so the following recipe is a good stand by.

My Florentines

7 ozs. sugar
5 ozs. self-raising flour
4 ozs. Scotts oats
3 ozs. coconut
2 ozs. sultanas
2 ozs. mixed chopped nuts
1 oz. cherries
Pinch of salt
4 ozs. margarine
2 dessert spoonsful Golden Syrup
1 egg

Method

Mix the dry ingredients together. Melt the margarine and syrup in a pan. Pour into the mixture and add the egg. Roll into small balls and space on a baking tray allowing room for the cakes to expand. When cool dip the bottom half in melted chocolate.

-August-

Everyone seems to be on holiday this month, everyone that is except Ronnie and me. We are still entertaining a stream of visitors to the garden, and when we get the chance, we love to stop and have a chat with them, finding out where they have come from and perhaps being able to offer them a tip or two to help them with their own gardens. By August, a lot of the vegetables are ready for harvesting, and again I have to say, praise be for the old freezer. If I can I like to make a start on some of the fruit wines.

You know, it really is a funny old life when you think about it, the chances are that I might be sweltering in the greenhouse and worrying about the possibility of a drought, yet at the same time I am thinking about the winter and planning what is to be done ready for it, and the first thing we have to do is get the spring cabbage seed planted this month. With the first of the apples being ready now, I thought I'd put this very old recipe for a pudding here.

Lammastide Pudding
(Lammas is 1st August.)

1/2 lb. short crust pastry
4 - 6 apples
1 teaspoonful cinnamon
1/2 pint single cream
2 eggs (separated)
2 ozs. butter
Castor sugar to taste

108

Method

Stew the apples with the cinnamon until tender. Add the remaining ingredients except for the egg whites.
Line a dish with short crust pastry, place the mixture into it and bake for 1/2 hour in a moderate oven.
Whip the egg whites to a solid froth. Pile on top of the pudding and pop into the oven until set.

-September-

This is the month when the fruit comes piling in and my house starts to look like a fruit storage depot, with buckets, pans, and any other container you can think of, full of damsons, apples, plums and pears. As well as making a lot of wine, I am a great one for jam making, so I will include a recipe here just in case that tree of yours should give you a bumper crop, or you decide to go into the country and 'pick your own' at a fruit farm. You know, there is nothing nicer than your own home-made jam on a piece of toast or bread and butter.

Plum Jam

(I use greengages, yellow plums, Early Rivers and Victorias.)

3 lbs. washed plums
3/4 pint water
3 lbs. sugar
1 piece of butter or margarine about the size of a walnut

Method

Put the plums and the water in a preserving pan, bring to the boil, reduce the heat and simmer until tender, about 10 - 15 minutes. Add the sugar and stir until dissolved. Bring it up to the boil again and boil hard for 10 - 15 minutes or until set. Draw the pan to one side away from the heat. Put the butter or

margarine into the pan and disperse the scum. Pot and cover.
This makes about 5 lbs. of jam.
I should have mentioned that I remove all the stones from the
plums before they go into the pan, but I also crack a few of the
stones and put the kernels in with the jam.

Marrow Cream

When you are tired of eating stuffed marrows, and have
made all the marrow jam that you want, why not try this recipe
as an alternative to lemon cheese.

2 lbs. marrow
2 lbs. lump sugar
4 ozs. butter
2 lemons

Method

Peel the marrow and boil it until it is quite soft. Strain well and
beat it to a pulp. Place in a saucepan with the sugar, butter,
juice and grated rind of the lemon. Boil slowly for about 3/4 of
an hour. This is a good filling for a tart.

Baked Carrot Pudding

1/2 lb. raw scraped carrots
1 lb. breadcrumbs
8 eggs
1/2 pint cream
4 ozs. melted butter
1/2 pint white wine
3 teaspoons of orange flower water
1 nutmeg (grated)
Short crust pastry (about 1/2 lb.)

Method

Beat the eight egg yolks with four of the whites and mix them into a cream. Stir in the grated carrots and breadcrumbs. Add the melted butter, wine flower water and nutmeg. Sweeten to taste. If too thick add a little milk or cream.
Line a dish with pastry and pour the carrot pudding mixture in. Bake in a very slow oven until set.
This is a very old Suffolk recipe dating from the time when eggs and cream were cheap and freely available.

While on the subject of vegetables, I don't know how useful you'll find this nowadays in the age of the freezer, but I still like to preserve some of my runner beans in salt. This is how we used to get over the problem of keeping them in my mother's day, and you know, I still think this method preserves the taste, I feel the frozen ones tend to be rather bland. At one time of day, I wouldn't have a freezer at any price, but then I saw the value of bulk buying, but for all that, I still think salting is the best way to preserve flavour.

Your runner beans should be gathered when they are still quite young and not more than three or four inches long. Have ready some clean dry jars - I often use old sweet jars with screw top lids. Roll some cooking salt until it is perfectly free from lumps. Put a layer of salt in the jar, then a layer of beans. Repeat until the jar is full, the top layer being one of salt. Tie down with parment or strong covers and store the jars in a very dry cupboard.
Note: Try not to use free flowing or iodised table salt. Use the old cooking block salt.

When you come to use your salted beans, put them to soak overnight in a bowl of water. The next morning put them into a saucepan of fresh water and bring them up to the boil. Immediately strain off all the water and then repeat this process twice, thus getting rid of all the salt. Then finally cook for 10 - 15 minutes, and you will find they are almost as good as fresh.

September being the month for harvest this is the time when

rabbits and hares abound, so I thought you might like a recipe for the way we cook hare in Suffolk.

Suffolk Hare

Hare is a strong meat, so after I have skinned mine, I leave to soak for two days in salt water, changing the water often. Cut the hare into joints. (If you are buying one from the butcher he will probably do this for you.)
You will need:-

A few mixed herbs in a small bag
Black pepper and salt
Fat to fry in
Flour for thickening
1/2 bottle red wine - I use home-made redcurrant or loganberry
Stock
Onions, carrots or any other root vegetable

Method

Put the flour and seasonings into a thick paper or polythene bag and then toss the joints into it making sure that they are thoroughly covered. Fry the joints in a little fat until they are well browned. I then fry the onions lightly. Then I put everything into a casserole with the wine, stock and herbs and cook at about 300 F for three hours.
Remove the bag of herbs just before serving. If you can also have some large well scrubbed potatoes baking down on the bottom shelf you have got yourself a perfect meal. Hares are in season from September through to February.

Beetroot Jelly

2 lbs. beetroot
1/2 pint white vinegar
6 cloves

6 peppercorns
1 small bayleaf
1/2 packet raspberry jelly

Method

Wash the beetroot, trim the stalks leaving about 1 inch. It is important not to cut away the root as the beetroot will bleed when cooking if the skin has been pierced. Boil the beet for about 1 1/2 hours or until tender. Cool and skin, then dice. Pack into jars. Place the vinegar and spices in a pan and cover. Bring to the boil and simmer for ten minutes. Strain, pour on to the jelly and allow it to dissolve completely. Cool but do not allow it to set. Pour over the beetroot covering it completely. When set, place a waxed paper disc in the jar and screw on the lid. It is better not to use tin lids, you can buy plastic lined ones.

- October -

"When onion skins are very thin, a mild winter's coming in. When onion skins are thick and tough, the coming winter's cold and rough."

By October most of the crops have been harvested. In the old days the corn harvest was much more of a village affair than it is now, because then every available pair of hands was brought in to help. The women having quickly done their chores at home, would join the men in the fields to help load up the wagons with the sheaves of corn. The young children came too, those old enough to help did so, the others played safely in a corner of the field. The farmer would provide a gallon of his home-brewed beer, and often there would be a hamper of food with home-made bread, pickled onions, a ham, rusks, applejacks and cakes of all descriptions. Around nine in the evening, perhaps, the work would be done,and as the last load was completed, it was the custom for the prettiest girl in the field to be placed on top of the load with a garland of corn and wild flowers on her head. Traditionally too, an oak bough was placed on the last load, and one sheaf was left standing in the field as a thank offering.

Of more recent origin is the Harvest Thanksgiving Service in church and village Harvest Supper. In our village we have a Harvest Horkey, held in one of the fruit houses of the local fruit farm. We put bales of straw for people to sit on round the sides of the fruit house and then we set up trestle tables to hold the food. Usually we have cold meats, beef, ham, turkey or pork and salads of everything you can think of. Some of the ladies of the committee responsible for the food even bring along with them baked potatoes which have been kept hot in foil. For puddings we have fruit tarts and cream and we wash it all down with beer and cider or tea and coffee. The place is decorated with autumn foliage, the bright berries from the hedgerows, and to add to the atmosphere we have hollowed out pumpkins with lighted candles inside. To round off our evening there will be some form of entertainment, perhaps a few sketches, some dancing by the children but above all else, a good old sing-song.

Here are a few ideas of what you could cook for your Harvest Supper, or you might like the recipes that date from the days when the farm workers spent all day out in the harvest field with only a snack to keep them going.

Fourses Cake

8 ozs. lard
2 lbs. self-raising flour
8 ozs. sugar
8 ozs. currants
Pinch of mixed spice
1 oz. yeast
1 pint milk

Method

Rub the lard into the flour. Add the sugar, currants and spices. Cream the yeast with a little sugar and mix with the milk. Stir into the dry ingredients. Leave to rise in a warm place for about an hour. Bake in a moderate oven for about half an hour.

This recipe was a great favourite of Ernie's and I often gave him Fourses in his lunch-box. It is one of those good old fashioned cakes which was ideally suited to being taken into the harvest field.

Harvest Loaf Cake

1 lb. self-raising flour
8 ozs. butter
12 ozs. soft brown sugar
4 eggs
1 teaspoon bicarbonate soda
Rind of lemon
A few glace cherries
2 teaspoons mixed spice
8 ozs. currants
4 ozs. mixed peel
8 ozs. sultanas
1/2 pint stout or ale

Method

Rub the fat into the flour, then add the rest of the dry ingredients except the bicarbonate of soda. Heat the stout, add the soda to it, mix quickly and while still frothy pour into a well in the centre of the dry ingredients. Add the eggs, well beaten. Pour the mixture into a lined cake tin and bake in a slow oven until firm to touch.

Pork and Marrow Pie

This is a very good stand by and often baked for Harvest Festival Suppers.

1 lb. lean pork
8 ozs. self-raising flour
About 6$\frac{1}{2}$ - 7 fl. ozs. of water
1 large onion
6 ozs. suet
1 medium marrow
$\frac{1}{4}$ teaspoon salt
1 small cooking apple

Method

Cut the meat into small cubes, slice the onion, peel and slice the apple. Lay these in a pie dish and cover with sliced marrow. Just cover with water and then with a piece of tin foil. Cook in a slow oven for 2 - 3 hours. Remove from the oven and allow to cool for three-quarters of an hour.
Make a pie crust of suet, flour, salt and water. Place on top of the pie and bake at 350 - 375 F for a further 30 minutes.

*

Of course at harvest time you have all those fruits and vegetables at hand just waiting to be turned into delicious pickles and chutneys which do so much to brighten up our plates during the winter. I'll just include a few of my favourite recipes here.

Quick Red Cabbage Pickle

1 red cabbage with a good heart
Salt
1 oz. black peppers to every 2 pints vinegar

Method

Remove outer leaves from the cabbage, cut out the middle stalk and then shred the cabbage finely. Spread on a dish, sprinkle with salt - 3 or 4 tablespoonsful for a medium sized cabbage. Leave for 24 hours. Place in a colander and drain well. Pack into jars.

Put the black peppercorns into a bit of muslin then place in the pan with the vinegar and bring to the boil. Skim well, then pour the cold spiced vinegar into the jars. Make air tight. This should be ready to eat in two weeks.

Runner Bean Chutney (Sweet)

2 lbs. trimmed and sliced runner beans
1¹/2 lbs. chopped onions
1 heaped tablespoon cornflour
1 heaped tablespoon turmeric
1 heaped tablespoon mustard
12 ozs. Demerara sugar
12 ozs. soft brown sugar
1¹/2 pints vinegar
Method

Prepare vegetables. Cook sliced beans in well-salted water until tender. Cook chopped onions in 1/2 pint vinegar. Strain beans, then add to the rest of the vinegar and cook for 10 minutes. Add sugar and rest of ingredients and boil for a further 12 - 15 minutes. Bottle and cover. This is a good recipe and keeps well.

Beetroot Chutney

1¹/2 lbs. beetroot
1 lb. apples
1 pint vinegar

1^{1}/$_{2}$ lbs. onions
1 lb. sugar
1/2 teaspoonful of ground ginger *(if liked)*

Method

Boil beetroot and peeled and chopped onions until tender in half the vinegar, the sugar, salt and ginger. Add the chopped apples and the rest of the vinegar. Boil for about half an hour. Allow to cool, then pot in the usual way.

Green Tomato Chutney

3 lbs. green tomatoes
4 large apples
2 small cucumbers
3 large onions
6 ozs. sultanas
12 ozs. brown sugar
2 tablespoons mustard
1^{1}/$_{2}$ teaspoons ground ginger
1 level teaspoon cayenne pepper
1^{1}/$_{2}$ tablespoons salt
4^{1}/$_{2}$ gills vinegar

Method

Remove the stalks from the tomatoes, slice and peel onions and apples. Slice the cucumbers and put all the ingredients into a large pan. Bring to the boil and simmer for two to three hours or until quite soft. Stir frequently. Put into warmed jars and seal down for at least two months.

- November -

We're almost back where we started in this chapter, with the mist and the cold, except that now the run up to Christmas starts in earnest, and I'm busy making Christmas cakes and mincemeat. This month we hold a Church Christmas Fair so there are pickles, jams and flower pictures to be made for that.

Quick Mincemeat (Makes about 5 - 6 lbs.)

8 ozs. raisins
6 ozs. mixed peel
12 ozs. sultanas
12 ozs. currants
1 1/2 lbs. peeled and cored cooking apples
4 ozs. suet
1 lb. brown sugar
Grated rind and juice of 1 lemon and 1 orange
2 teaspoonsful mixed spice
1/2 teaspoonful ground cinnamon
1 teaspoonful ground nutmeg
6 tablespoonsful rum or sherry

Method

Mix together the fruit and apples, then mix in the sugar, suet and spices. Finally add the juice and sherry or rum. Pack into jars and cover.

Christmas Pudding (Makes 4)

1 lb. sultanas
1 lb. raisins
1 lb. currants
1 lb. Demerara or moist brown sugar
8 ozs. mixed peel
8 ozs. suet

119

1 lb. freshly made breadcrumbs
1 lb. plain flour
8 ozs. almonds
1/2 teaspoon salt
2 teaspoonsful ground nutmeg
2 teaspoonsful ground cinnamon
2 teaspoonsful mixed spice
6 eggs
1 pint of stout
2 medium grated apples
2 medium grated carrots

Method

Chop the nuts, then mix all the ingredients together. Don't forget to let all the family make a wish as they have a stir of the pudding. Place the mixture into four fairly large basins, covered with greased paper then tie on a cloth.
I boil my puddings in my electric copper for 4 - 5 hours the day after I have made them, that allows them to mature a bit. When they are cooked I put fresh cloths on them, and then, on the day they are required I steam them for another 3 hours.

Christmas Cake

I like to make this early because the taste mellows and improves with a little time. My mum loved this cake and this is really her recipe.

8 ozs. currants
8 ozs. stoned raisins, chopped
4 ozs. mixed peel
1 grated rind of lemon
1 tsp. baking powder
1 level tsp. mixed spice
1 level tsp. ground cinnamon
6 small eggs

1 lb. sultanas
6 ozs. glace cherries
2 ozs. blanched almonds
10 ozs. plain flour
Pinch of salt
1 level tsp. ground nutmeg
10 ozs. butter
10 ozs. dark brown sugar

120

2 level dessp. black treacle   2 tbsp. rum or brandy
Little milk for mixing if needed   8" square tin

Method

Line the tin with tinfoil or greaseproof paper.
Mix all the fruit together with the chopped almonds and lemon rind. Sift the flour, baking powder and spices with the salt. Cream the butter and sugar, then beat in the eggs gradually, then the black treacle. Finally stir in the fruit with the sifted dry ingredients, the rum and the milk if necessary. Turn the mixture into the prepared tin, smooth the surface and hollow out the centre slightly so that the cake will level when baked.
Place in the centre of a warm oven about 325 F. After $1/2$ an hour turn the heat down to 300 F for $31/2$ hours.
To see if the cake is cooked, press a thin warm skewer into the centre and if it comes out clean, the cake is done. If it sticks to the skewer put it back for another ten minutes or so. Leave the cake in the tin for an hour before turning it on a cooling tray. I also leave the paper on until I am ready to ice the cake. I wrap the cake thoroughly and then store it in a tin with a closed lid with an apple. There is a lovely smell when you take the cake out.

After all that rich food cooking, here's a lovely savoury dish for a November supper.

Aldeburgh Sprats

Wash the sprats well, (the number will depend on how many you like) dry them and then dust them with fine oatmeal. Sprinkle a frying pan with salt, heat the pan and then put in the sprats and fry them until they are golden brown. There is no need to put fat in the pan as the salt draws out the fat from the fish.
    This was a favourite dish of my dad, and mum used to add chopped parsley.

- December -

What a busy month this is, although for me it is not quite as busy as it has been in the past, as there were turkeys and chickens to be dressed for friends and neighbours, this meant plucking them, removing the entrails and generally getting them ready for the oven. Nowadays there is less demand and most people seem happy to buy 'Oven Ready' birds from the supermarkets. So over the years this tradition for me has ceased. Ernie used to take a day of his holiday just before Christmas so that he could help with lifting the vegetables and cutting the logs for the fires. He would also help me by delivering a few small parcels around to some of the older people in the village, some home-made cakes, a bottle of home-made wine and some Christmas decorations.

We start the real Christmas Festivities with the Candle-lit Carol Service on the Sunday before Christmas. We decorate the church with greenery and flowers, we have a Christmas tree and of course there is the crib. It is lovely to join with all my friends to sing the old and well-loved carols and to think of what the season really celebrates.

On the afternoon of Christmas Eve I stuff my turkey. We usually have a twenty pound bird. Sometimes I am lucky enough to be given a pheasant, so I dress that and put it right inside the turkey. I stuff the turkey breast with chestnut stuffing and in the other end I use a forcemeat stuffing. I put rashers of bacon all over the top of the bird, then wrap it up in foil and half cook it in the oven while we go to Midnight Service. I also make a sherry trifle, a fruit salad and finish icing my buns.

Chestnut Stuffing

1 lb. chestnuts
8 ozs. chopped ham or bacon

1 teacup fresh breadcrumbs
2 ozs. butter
Little chopped parsley
Little stock or milk to bind

Method

Prick the nuts and boil in water for 15 - 20 minutes. When cool, remove the skins. Rub through a sieve, or put in the liquidiser for a few seconds. Add to the other ingredients and mix thoroughly.

Forcemeat Stuffing

2 ozs. fresh parsley
4 ozs. fresh breadcrumbs
2 ozs. suet
2 ozs. fresh thyme
Grated rind of 1/2 lemon
Pepper and salt to taste
1 egg
2 small rashers bacon (chopped)

Method

Mix all the ingredients together and bind with the beaten egg. You can vary this recipe using mushrooms or sausage. Dried herbs can be used if you haven't any fresh ones available.

As soon as I step inside the church late on Christmas Eve, I forget all the rushing around and the feverish preparations, and there is that peace which we all look forward to in that magical, mystical Midnight Communion Service. If my family are with me for the service, then that is even better. Christmas has always been the time when our whole family got together, and in their last years we all tried to make it as nice as possible for mum and dad. Mum used to work so very hard for us, it was but a trifle we could do to thank her. She made Christmas, and

123

when we lost her, it took on another shape, since I'm the mother now.

After the Midnight Service, where perhaps there is a congregation of forty or fifty, we come home to a late supper of ham and pickle, bread rolls and cheese, before we go to bed around 2.30 a.m.

Nowadays we have a leisurely breakfast, for those who want it, about half past nine, but I bet you would have been surprised at what my dad liked to have for breakfast on Christmas morning - a Rabbit Pie! Now, I'm sure that none of you would think of eating such a thing at such a time, but I'll give you the recipe now and then you might like to try it some other time.

Dad's Rabbit Pie

1 nice young rabbit
12 ozs. fat bacon or pork
Salt and pepper
A little dripping
4 ozs. onions
1/2 pint stock or water
About 1/2 lb. short crust pastry

Method

Cut up the rabbit and bacon or pork. Melt the dripping in a pan and lightly fry the onion and meats for about 5 - 10 minutes. Sprinkle with salt and pepper, add the stock or water, then simmer gently for three-quarters of an hour or so. Leave until cold, then fill the pie dish with the meat, add the stock, cover with pastry and bake in a moderate oven for about 11/2 hours. If liked, just before the pie is cooked, take it out of the oven and brush it with a little milk to give it a nice finish.

During the morning, while the cooking is looking after itself, I like to take a walk around the garden, and usually I find a few fresh flowers there if the autumn has been mild. Perhaps two or three roses, just to give that final touch to the dining table. We have our Christmas dinner at about 1.30p.m. and only then do we open our presents. But before that there is the 10.30 church service in which the children take part. Afterwards it is more than likely friends and relations will call in for a drink and hot mince pies. At this time of year there is nothing nicer than a good mulled wine.

Mulled Wine

1/4 pint water
1 level teaspoonful nutmeg
1/2 level teaspoonful ground cinnamon
4 tablespoonsful Demerara sugar
Thinly peeled rind of 1 lemon and 1 orange
2 bottles home-made wine - apple or any fruit wine
6 tablespoonsful liqueur, brandy or sherry

Method

Simmer the water, spices, sugar and citrus rinds for about 35 minutes to get good flavours. Strain and return to the heat, then add the wine and liqueur. Heat very gently but do not allow to boil. Serve hot, but don't forget to put a spoon in the glass as you pour to prevent the glass cracking.

An alternative is this very pleasant Wine Cup which can also be served at buffet parties.

Wine Cup

1 bottle white wine
3 wine glasses sherry
1 measure of brandy
1 large bottle lemonade

Method

Mix all the ingredients together and serve.

*

Here's a recipe that is a mixture of food and drink! It's a very old dish that was traditionally eaten on Christmas Eve.

Frumenty

Boil 1 pint of wheat in water or milk flavoured with mixed spice and then thickened slightly with flour. You can add raisins, nutmeg and cinnamon and eggs and cream. If you add dried fruit, then it has always been considered best to boil it first. On special occasions rum or brandy was stirred into the dish. When everything is mixed together leave it to set.

To end the year I'll give you an old Suffolk recipe. This was given to me by a very old lady who had at one time been the maid to the Rector of Laxfield. This recipe is thought to date from 1860 and was often made for dinner parties.

Potato Pudding

1/2 lb. prepared potatoes
1/2 lb. butter
1/2 lb. castor sugar
6 eggs
glass of brandy

Method

Boil the potatoes until soft, mash them and then rub through a sieve until fine and smooth. Melt the butter and beat in the sugar. Beat the eggs and stir them into the other ingredients

126

with the glass of brandy. Put into a greased pudding basin and steam for about half an hour.

So there you have a glimpse into some of the things that come out of my kitchen during the year. As the 31st of December draws to a close we look back at what we have achieved during the past year and look forward to all those things we hope to do as the New Year dawns and for good measure as a symbol of what is to come, I like to get out into the greenhouse to plant some seeds to start the whole thing off.

AKENFIELD

Ronald Blythe has been a neighbour and a very good friend of ours for years. Like us he is a Suffolk person and knows the life of our area, which led him to write the Book 'Akenfield' which describes how the changes of the last eighty year have affected not only the farmers and farm workers, but teachers and clergymen, doctors and nurses, in fact, every single one of us. The book proved to be a best-seller, and I enjoyed it very much. I was only involved in the book itself insofar as I suppose I'm a typical Suffolk girl and mother, and so anyone writing about life here could draw on me as an example.

I shall always remember that particular day. It was the 4th February and I had been to church on my own that morning as Ernie and the boys were not feeling too well. As I was leaving after the service, Ronald stopped me and said he would like a word with me. We just stopped there, on the path, to chat, as I thought, about going to some church meeting, when out of the blue he said, "Peggy, would you like to be the mother in the film of my book?" Well, you could have knocked me down! I said, "But Ronald, I've never acted in my life." This didn't seem to concern him, he simply said, "Well you think it over and go home and talk it over with Ernie and the boys." He went on to say that Peter Hall had seen me last year at the flower show and had said then that he had thought I would be right for the part but he added, "he will want you to have a film test." You can imagine what was going through my mind as I went home from church that morning!

As I was getting the Sunday dinner out, I said, very casually, "Ronald has asked me to be in his film." With that the boys roared with laughter and David said. "Coo, mum, you're only good for gardening, and if you go in for that film your old head will swell and you'll need a bigger door to get through!" Ernie, on the other hand, was very understanding, and said; "If you've got a chance to do something you would like to do, you have a go at it."

About three days later I had a 'phone call from a young man called Garrow Shand who said he had been asked to pick me up on 14th February to take me to London to have this film test. I had known Garrow, who was born and bred in Suffolk, for years as my mother and his nanny were great friends from the days when they had been next door neighbours in Cambridgeshire, and we would often meet when we visited 'Aunt Phoebe' as we used to call her. Of recent years we had often seen Garrow go through the village on his tractor as he was a contractor for ploughing or muck spreading for the farmers around Charsfield and other villages.

As we talked I asked Garrow how he had come to get his part in the film, and he said he had simply answered an advertisement in the local paper which had asked for people who were interested in taking part in a Suffolk film. He had had an interview at a school in Woodbridge and been picked for the part of my son.

At 10 o'clock on St. Valentines Day, Garrow arrived to pick me up. I had to smile to myself afterwards as I had got my best suit on and had made extra sure that I looked my best, but when I got into his van, Garrow moved aside some old sacks and some oil drums saying, "I hope you don't mind, but this is my only van and I have to use it for carting everything in." We certainly didn't look like my idea of a couple setting out for a film test. Of course, that had to be the morning that we had the first snow of the winter and at times it was snowing so hard we couldn't see out of the windows, a rum old blizzard! Garrow thought it would be best if we took the train from Ipswich to Liverpool Street, and as we did not have to be in London until 2 o'clock we had plenty of time. When we did arrive in London, I was very glad that Garrow was with me as I didn't know much about the place, but he soon found us a taxi to take us to the address we had for the producers home in the Notting Hill area.

I had naturally thought that the screen test would be held in a

129

big place with a large studio, but I could not have been more off the mark, it was simply a room with some cameras and video equipment set up around us. But the producer was a very friendly man, though he did look more like a down-and-out than a successful film producer! As the year went on I got used to him looking like this. But he was certainly a contrast to Peter Hall, who was a very smart gentleman, dressed that day in a splendid black coat with a velvet collar. When I first met him, I wondered why such a man as he should be so interested in making this particular film, but he told me that he too was a Suffolk man and that he wanted to express his love for the place. He said that when he had read the book he felt that it was just like listening to his grandfather talking, and that it had had a great emotional effect upon him.

The third person present for the test was Barbara Tilney, a young school-teacher, now working in London, but originally from Beccles. She too had got the part as a result of answering an advertisement.

By this time I was beginning to feel nervous. We were told to sit round the table which had been set out with tea things. Peter then told us the background to the story. I was a widow, Garrow was my son Tom, and Barbara was to be Tom's girlfriend Jean. I was then asked by Peter to imagine that my son had been out all night and I was to ask him what he thought he was up to. Well I looked at Garrow, and then at Barbara, and then I talked the biggest squit on earth for about an hour and a half! Then Peter said, "That will do. We will be in touch with you all." I remember saying to him, "Well, I am what I am and I can't put no airs and graces on for nobody." (One of my pet hates is someone trying to put on the posh talk or speaking as if they'd got a plum stuck in their mouth.) But Peter said, "Don't you change at all. We want you as Suffolk people."

As Garrow and I sat on the train home, I said, "What do you think about it all, then?" He remarked that they seemed a rum old lot, but we'd have to wait and see what they all turned out like. I said we could only do our best, but really we had no

130

idea how a film was made or how these people were going to set about it.

On 19th February I heard that I had got the part in the film, that the film company was hoping to start ten days later, and also that they would be in touch with me. Two days later Ronald Blythe invited me to go and have tea with him and he told me some of the things they were hoping to do. He also said that the company would like my help in those scenes which required food. I felt a bit easier in my mind after seeing Ronald as he had explained that there wouldn't be any lines as such to learn, it would all be 'ad lib' as far as possible. He also asked me to help out with the odd bit of running about until the film crew got to know their way around. Ronald can't drive so he could not do this for them. He also explained that all the filming would take place at weekends as Peter Hall had the National Theatre to see to, as well as the crew having their jobs to do in the week. Later that week Rex, the producer, rang me from London to say that they were hoping to make a start on 3rd March at Debach old school with a scene set in 1906 and would I be able to help dress the children in their old-fashioned costumes. He also told me that the company had hired an empty farmhouse at Burgh as a sort of headquarters in which to store the props and so on.

The day arrived when we all met. The first to arrive and introduce herself to me was the secretary, a nice little girl called Jenny, but far too thin in my opinion. I thought as I looked at her, 'a good meal wouldn't do you any harm, Missie.' She was in a bit of a flap as she was trying to organise the next day's filming. It was to be a farmyard scene and she needed two more farm workers. I told her that I was sure Ernie and Allan would help out if she thought they would do..

My main job was to help the children get ready and as soon as I saw them dressed I went and got my own camera and I thought to myself it would be a long time before I ever saw anything like that again. The children, with Jean looking so stern, made me think of a picture out of an old Dickens novel. It was a

Old Tom ploughing - 'Akenfield'

bitter cold day and we were all perishing cold standing in that old school porch listening to Jean as she scolded the children for being late.

The next morning Peter wanted to have the children back up at the school as the light had not been right and he wanted to re-take the scene. I went to pick up the children, but when I went to get one of the little boys who had cried in the school the day before, his mum said, "I don't know if he will come with you as he don't like that old teacher. He's even been dreaming about her." However we got him into the car, but as soon as he saw the school, he started to howl. We had to bribe him with sweets and books to get him inside, and then I sat with him on my knee drawing pictures in his book until they were ready for him in the classroom. It was a touching scene.

Later in the day I went with Ernie and Allan to Miss Bennett's farm at Burgh where the men were supposed to be having their bait or whittles. I had been asked to find some bread, cheese and fat bacon for this scene. I had given the men their food and while they were waiting for the camera men to turn up, they had a bit of a rehearsal using a 'shut' knife and thumb technique on the whittles. Of course, by the time the crew arrived they'd eaten the blessed lot. I soon learnt by that mistake, and no food was given out after that until the producer shouted "action".

On 10th March came the scene at the forge in Burgh where we had met for the first time the late Mr Stanley Baxter, a dear old Suffolk 'character'. He didn't think much of Peter Hall at first as he asked the old boy to use a swear word. I was particularly interested in this scene as the Arts Director had got three or four large bales of peat ready to cover over the tarmac road surface thus giving the impression of the unmade roads of the 1900s. He said that I could have all the peat for my garden when they had finished with it, but I think that it had been watered to kingdom come by the time they had filmed that scene. The farm workers were supposed to be sheltering in the forge from the rain, so Peter had the men standing under a barn with a hosepipe dripping on them, but then he said, "Sorry

The committal of Old Tom - 'Akenfield'

Ronald Blythe the author of 'Akenfield'
who also played the part of the rector in the film

chaps, you're not getting wet enough," so he got them to stand in the middle of the road near the forge and hired a fire engine from Ipswich to provide the downpour, and the men were duly drenched. Then if you please, after all that, the light was so bad they couldn't shoot the film that day, so he asked the 'chaps' to come back next day. After a lot of muttering a bottle of whisky was produced and the men agreed to return. The following day they went through the same procedure, so you can see why it was I couldn't sweep the peat up.

The following morning we went over to Great Glenham, near Saxmundham, to see the horse ploughing scene. We had laughed to ourselves as the crew had said they were going to be up early and do an early scene. I said, "What do you call 'early'? Not 9 a.m. I hope." When we arrived it was what we call a rare old morn, hoary frost and a bit of fog. Mr. Clark from Nayland had already arrived with his horses. Then Tom turned up and said he couldn't plough with them as he was only used to a tractor. My husband, who had done ploughing with horses in his younger days, volunteered to open a few furrows for Tom to carry on. Then we discovered that Tom's clothes had been forgotten, so back home we went to undress the scarecrow to provide Tom with a mac, scarf and hat!

It was a rough old field that one where old sows had been rooting, but Peter seemed pleased with the mornings work and on the film it looks very effective with the mist lifting off the ground.

After a weekend of filming it was quite common to see Ronald cycling round looking for suitable sites for later filming. He must have cycled miles and miles looking for just the right views and locations.

The following week Ronald asked me if I could think of any lady in the village who would take the part of a stone picker. He said he wanted someone who looked as if she had come down in the world. Well, can you imagine telling any lady that! I thought of several possibilities, but I knew they really wanted someone rather tall. I approached someone, she came along the next weekend. Peter said she would be suitable, so the stone

Charlotte and Tom Courting - 'Akenfield'

picking scene was done there and then. Poor woman, she told me afterwards she had worked jolly hard picking them old stones up and would not like to do that job for a living.

The same weekend they filmed the 1943-45 dance scene for which they had found a girl who was supposed to be ma as an 18 year old. They had two ladies cutting all the men's hair the day before filming, even my son who was playing an Air Force chap agreed to have his cut to the length that was usual in those days. Ernie and I spent the weekend looking for a chapel suitable to film the baptism scene. Although we went miles afield, we ended up in a chapel at Woodbridge.

During the last week in March Rex rang from London to ask, "Peggy, can you find us a baby for next week?" By now I was used to being asked to find some peculiar thing, but that, I thought, takes the biscuit. Once more I put on my thinking cap and wondered who on earth I could ask to loan their baby, not just for one weekend, if I knew anything about the way this filming business worked. As it turned out, it was for three. I asked several mothers but, understandably, they didn't think much of the idea, then, the mum of the little boy who had cried in the school scene let us have his baby brother on condition that I looked after him. So that's what I did, feeding and changing him between shots. It was just like old times again.

At the little cottage in Henley where we had the baby it was once more back in the days of the hard times of the 1900s. Tom was taking the part of his grandfather. I had gone over with the Arts Director to help him with some items for the cottages, pots and pans and so on, and my aspidistra plant, so fashionable in those days and now back again in fashion, and my grandmother's white bed cover.

A funny thing happened in this scene. Charlotte, Tom's wife, was supposed to be making a rabbit stew. They needed a rabbit and I had to find one and skin it as Charlotte could not do it. I was all right for two weekends but when I tried to get a rabbit for the third one, I couldn't find one anywhere. Then as I went along the road, I saw a rabbit sitting by the roadside. I stopped the car and could see at a glance that the poor thing had got

Myxomatosis. I picked it up, looked up and down the road to see if there was anyone about then wrung its neck quickly. I felt that in fact I was doing the poor thing a kindness as its head was twice the normal size. I took it back to the cottage without a word about where I'd got it, then I skinned it and nobody was any the wiser. It wasn't eaten, of course.

Ian, the Arts Director, was a very kind man and the following week he came to me and said, "Now Peggy, come down and see the little cottage that we've started to get ready for you." The little cottage was at Letheringham and when I saw it, I got such a surprise, for Ian had been to a sale and managed to furnish the place from top to bottom. All I had to do was find the bits and pieces like photo frames, brass ornaments, the iron and so on. So that by the time we had finished the place looked really like a home that was being lived in. Many's the time while we were filming I had to go and get my iron or some other utensil that I needed to use but had been left in my 'other cottage'.

The house had not been lived in for two years so the garden was completely overgrown. Undaunted, Ernie and I went down and made an instant garden in a week. He dug a patch up at the side of the cottage and using the thinnings out from our own garden we made up rows of vegetables, and we sowed radishes, peas and beans, hoping they would be up when they filmed shots outside the cottage later in the summer. Ian and I also went to a nursery garden and bought climbing roses to go over the front door, small roses and flowering plants. A bit of paint was put on the gate, and the whole place looked quite smart when it was done.

I started my part in the film on 15th April. It was the kitchen scene at breakfast time. I was feeling a bundle of nerves, which was good as it happened, because Peter told me that I was supposed to be in a flap trying to get so much done in a little time. This was the scene where I had to be riled with Tom for coming in late. I had got the kitchen all set out and had been told to cook two eggs and bacon. Poor old Tom, I felt sorry for him as I cooked those eggs and bacon six times and he had to

Peter Hall filming 'Akenfield'

eat the lot! He told me that each time they stopped filming he shot outside and was sick as he never eats fried stuff. I felt awful about this because they were large rashers. I was so worried by the end of that Sunday that we were doing something wrong, but as time went on I realised that this was the way they worked, doing the same scene over and over and then picking out the one that was best.

There was to be no filming the next weekend as it was Easter, so I got in a good week's baking. The funeral scene was coming up and I had been asked if I could provide a few cakes. I have never been know to buy a cake for my family, so I had a high old time making fruit cakes, sausage rolls, Suffolk rusks, and coffee and chocolate gateaux. I also pickled a ham. At least with cooking I knew where I was and I didn't have to repeat everything like I did when we filmed the scene of my reading the letter from the former Rector of the parish who had known Tom's grandfather. I think I must have read it at least nine times before I got it right. Then there was the part where I had to take Tom's shirt and tie to his bedroom and I find him sitting on the bed reading his emigration papers. I must have walked to that bedroom door and opened it a score of times. I knew by the expression on Peter's face when he shouted "Cut!" that I hadn't got it right.

I still hadn't got it right when we resumed filming on 5th May. Four more times I had to read that blessed letter. Then I had to tell Jean that I had seen Tom with the papers for New Zealand. It was a very trying day and I think we must all have had 20 cups of tea during that time.

We all met at Hoo Church on 11th May for the funeral scene. We walked in and out of the church eight or nine times. I felt awful as it bought back so many sad memories of my poor old dad for next to the church was the farm where dad had worked as a boy then finished his last years there. When they sang the hymn 'The day thou gavest Lord, is ended' my heart quite turned over. I could feel the tears coming, it was dad's funeral all over again right down to that hymn. I was glad when we finished that day and I don't think I shall ever forget that part, it was so real. The next day I had a small bottle of brandy in my bag to help see me through.

On that occasion there were over 100 people at the church with over 80 young men from Framlingham College dressed as First World War soldiers. There were others all dressed in period clothes who were grandfather's mates, farm workers, stone pickers and so on.

Next we moved on to Mr Holland's farm at Pettistree where we saw Tom with all the up-to-date machinery. We also saw Ted and his mates having their bait and Ted telling the story of how old Tom had been taken short one day and gone in a ditch. As he came out he discovered he couldn't stand up straight. "My back's gone!" he yelled and was somewhat taken aback when Ted yelled back with a laugh, "You silly old fool, you've gone and done your braces up to your fly buttons."

My family were indirectly involved in the next scene which was of old Tom and Robin in the churchyard at Hoo. Robin was a grave digger but he could not stop to dig the grave for the film scene, so Ronald asked Ernie if he could do it. With Allan's help the job was done in the evening, but that was the only time I'd ever known Ernie to dig a grave and have no body to go in it. There was another time when Robin was needed for a scene and he also had a grave to fill in over at Kesgrave. I told him not to worry and to get on with the film and I would go and start filling in the grave for him. It wouldn't, I assured him, be the first time I had helped to fill in a grave.

We went next to Mr. Anderson's farm at Boulge for the sheep dipping scene. Mr. B. Wilson brought over some of his sheep and what they thought about it all I don't know. 17th May was rather early for this job as dipping is usually done at the end of June when the fly is about.

Then it was back to the cottage for a chat about the funeral scene with the arrival of Ted, Molly and Charlie. And of course, Aunt Ida. Now she had come into the film quite by accident. Her husband had come to try for a part and Peter had spotted her and liked the look of her face. He told Ronnie that he wanted her in somewhere so it was decided that she should be old Tom's sister.

This section of the film was going to take some time so we had all taken a week's holiday to get on with it. I had made all the preparations for the funeral meal and the table was laid with plenty of food and six bottles of wine, but as it poured with rain we had to pack up early as the light was too bad for filming.

But next day, in true English fashion, it was a lovely morning with the sun shining when we all met at the cottage. There were fourteen people, all of them supposed to be relations. It was just like a party - my six bottles of wine didn't go anywhere so I sent Ernie home to get some more, and somehow six gallons of wine went west - and the faces began to get red. I think that the crew had their fair share too, the stories that were told that day were never to be forgotten - we laughed till we cried. Peter had asked Aunt Ida to say she remembered her brother getting wed in the harvest field, she thought he said, getting wet in the harvest field. Poor old girl, she had had her share of the wine for the men kept filling up her glass till she didn't know if she was coming or going.

On the following day we went in the funeral cars to the church. We rode round and round the village and up and down the lanes. As we passed a cottage on the way to the church I remember seeing two chaps painting it. As we passed them one took off his cap and they both stood very reverently and respectful. We had to go by them three times and on the third occasion Ted told the driver to stop and he leaned out and shouted, "It's all right mate, he ain't quite dead yet!" You should have seen the look on their faces.

But filming isn't all laughs by any means. We walked up to that church door at least a dozen times and it was quarter to seven before we finished that night. It had been a very warm day and I was tired right out. So in many ways I was very glad that the next day I would have a change of routine. Right at the outset of the film I had told Rex that I would not be available on the 25th May as I had promised to arrange the flowers in the

143

church at Wickham Market for a friend's wedding. I was halfway through two large pedestal arrangements when Richard, another Arts Director and a real Christian man, walked into church and said that I was needed at the cottage to do a small scene. Poor man, I could see that he hardly liked to ask but he explained that that was the way the film world worked. When we got to the cottage where Ted and Molly were waiting to do the little scene of Ted bringing me the cups from the village hall it was 11 o'clock, but there was no sign of the film crew. They eventually turned up at about 2 p.m. having spent the morning filming Tom walking in the countryside. It was five before we had finished and I could get back to Wickham Market with a splitting headache to finish my flowers.

The next day was a complete day off though, for not only did we attend our friend's wedding, but in the evening we went to have dinner at Melton Grange with Rex and all the crew. How nice it was, just for once to be waited on and not even have to think about the washing-up

While I was living in another world, in the real one my son Allan had finished his school days in late June and had his first interview for joining the Police as a Cadet. At this time too, Ronald and I often used to talk about the harvest scenes which they were hoping to film at the end of August. I had been asked if I could help with finding old craftsmen who knew how the harvesting was done in 1912, and also to find equipment and implements. Then there was the problem of finding about forty people for the harvest scenes. Rex had already explained that they could not use me in any of the harvest scenes but he asked if I would be willing to help with the catering for the crew and actors. He added that they intended to hire a caravan in which I could prepare the food. So there I was at home baking and cooking joints of beef and pork and making pies and I don't know what.

By this time too, our garden was looking very pretty and Anglia TV came for the day to film it for the programme Garden Choice. It was just like being used for filming

Akenfield once more. I often think of how they poured water on the roses and shook it off to make it look like morning dew.

I was kept pretty busy during July as I had two more churches to decorate for weddings and we were receiving visitors to see the garden by the bus load. Sometimes it would be a Women's Institute outing or a Women's Club from the towns out for a mystery tour ending up at our garden. It was on 11th August that we heard that we had won the Council House Garden Shield for the best kept garden for the third time.

In the middle of August I went to tea with Ronnie to talk over the plans for the harvest filming. Peter had made plans last year for a farmer in Clopton to sow two fields of winter barley for the film and then he would pick the best one for use. My job was to provide an old basket filled with food for the women to take into the fields for the menfolk's tea-break or fourses, as they called it. Of course, I was also to provide the food. Ronnie said they need to be made from the old recipes. I knew this was a challenge but it would be nice to cook some of the old-fashioned dishes. As beer was also needed, I made up three gallons of home brew.

Akenfield's harvest started on 18th August, a lovely bright day. All the men and women, about thirty all told, arrived looking most realistic in their costumes. We also had nine or ten children. Ted and Molly's little son David who was four and a half wanted to be in the scene too, but they hadn't any clothes for him, so I slipped back home and found an old pair of trousers and a shirt which had been my David's and Sally, the Arts Dresser, cut them to size for him. The trouble was that the only boots we could find for him were about four sizes too big. Poor little mite, he looked so forlorn.

Soon the men had started to mow the field, tying up the barley and standing it up in stocks. Then Ernie noticed that they had no bags to carry the rubs for sharpening the scythes. These small bags are fixed to the belts of the reapers. Ernie came home and got some old rubber boots and cut them down to make the necessary bags. The old reaping machine that was used came from Easton Farm Park; it had been rebuilt and reconditioned by Clifford Arbon, a wheelwright from the next village.

In my mind the harvest was one of the high points of the film, and it was very moving when the last loaded carts were drawn past the 'big house' to show the master that the harvest was done. (Ernie had gone to Clopton earlier in the day to take over two loads of corn for this scene.) As the long procession of workers filed past the house, some of the men carried lanterns to show how late the workers of days gone by used to work. As they walked they sang and the young lads shouted 'Largesse, Largesse' the cry of a harvest done and beer money wanted as a reward. We came right back to the present though when Richard went and got fish and chips for all the actors as it was so late when the scene was done.

It was a sad day when we met to do the last scene where we were all together. This was Jean's baptism which was filmed at the chapel in Woodbridge. It was a very moving moment when Jean went down into the water. On a brighter note was a gift of a bottle of champagne from the crew to Ernie for his birthday the following day.

It had been a wonderful experience, we had made so many friends, but work and life had to go on even though it was rather strange at first. I felt there was something missing about the place as we had got so used to various members of the crew popping in for tea or help with maps for going from one village to another.

But we did have the premiere to look forward to. And that came in mid-November. It was pouring with rain when we left and our street was flooded for the first time in years. Allan was on a week's leave so he came home to look after David and the animals and my mum looked in on them every day. Ernie and I had been invited to spend the weekend in Surrey with Richard and his mother, before going to spend a week in a London hotel at the expense of the film company.

On Monday, 18th November we met Rex and Ronald for lunch and then went to a reception at the Martine Terrace to launch the 18th London Film Festival. After that we went back to the hotel to meet Ted and Molly. The hotel was the land of luxury to us, a porter to carry our bags and a man at the desk who asked me what time I would like tea in the morning. I told him, "At home I always have my tea at 6 a.m." He looked at me and laughed, "Well, madam, if you want it that early, then you will have to get the staff up and take them tea!" Then there were the lifts, we wouldn't forget them in a hurry as they went up and down so fast. We were standing there by the door and Ted just stepped in to see how it worked, when the doors closed and away he went. Molly and I got in the next lift to see if we could find him, but in the meantime Ted had gone back down again to look for us. It was a good fifteen minutes before we all caught up with each other. How that hall porter laughed at us.

Our rooms were right at the top with a wonderful view overlooking Hyde Park. And what a room, with a bathroom and colour television and a 'phone to ring if we wanted anything. I could not take it all in. We had never been to stay in a hotel before, so you can guess how we felt. We each had a lovely hot bath - no worrying about paying for the hot water, and then we met Ted and Molly for tea. A pot of tea, four sandwiches and four cakes cost £5 (I dread to think what they would charge nowadays). Ted looked at Ernie and said, "Bor, we shan't last long up here with a tenner. After this lot we shan't have the fare to get home."

At 8 p.m. we were picked up by taxi and taken to the National Film Theatre. My reaction to the film was 'where was it all'" So much was missing. But what really surprised me was that I had such a big part in the film, and that really was me up there, in colour, in close up and in so much detail.

After the film showing we had a party that was out of this world. We met so many people and real film stars, and in a way, it was just as confusing to see them in the flesh as it was to see myself on film. Neither is quite real, and it was all sort of topsy turvy.

But Ted bought us back down to earth when at half past two

in the morning we walked up to London Bridge to look for a taxi and he said, "I wish I had bought my old tractor." Six hours later we all met for breakfast before Ted and Molly set off back to their farm.

Ernie and I went exploring, finding our way by Underground to Madame Tussaud's and walking down Oxford Street looking in the shop windows. We returned to the hotel to have a quiet meal on our own. It came to nearly £20. We nearly had a fit - I thought, my goodness, that's two week's housekeeping money - but it was a wonderful meal and we had been told to have just what we wanted.

The rest of our time in London was a whirl of colour. There was the Royal Horticultural Show with plants with names I'd never seen or heard of before; shopping in the large stores; lunch with Rex in Hyde Park, and finally we were the guests of Lord Birkett at the House of Lords where the second reading of the Bill on the National Theatre was taking place. I can tell you, the sights and colours of London were marvellous, but I don't envy anyone living there. It is like a constant kaleidoscope, with thousands of shapes and colours, when all you want most of the time is one or two comforting colours.

The big day finally came when Akenfield was shown on television. It was seen, so we were told, by more than twelve million people! After we had watched ourselves that night, our telephone didn't stop ringing with people wishing to congratulate us. And never in my life have I had so much post, letters came from all over the country - hundreds of them, I even had one from the bishop.

The village had mixed feelings about the film. Some had thought it was going to be just like the book, while others could not understand the switchbacks in time. But on the whole most people enjoyed it. The local press called it 'A classic, down to earth story of a Suffolk village' and gave great praise to Peter Hall and Ronald Blythe. There were of course letters in the papers, some good and some criticising ones, so I had a busy time cutting them all out and I ended up with two large books full of them.

Then I had letters asking me to open fetes and flower shows, and to do the honours at prize givings. I just couldn't believe it was all happening to me, just an ordinary Suffolk girl.

In the New Year it was suggested that those of us who had been in the film should give Rex a present. We had seen more of him than any of the crew - if we wanted to know anything it was always 'ask Rex'. We eventually bought him a very nice Suffolk chair and we had a brass plate put on it engraved with the message, 'To Rex, from all his Suffolk friends while making Akenfield.' At this time too, I was presented with a handsome silver ring and a pendant with an amethyst in it, engraved on the back with Akenfield. I treasure both these as they were given to me by Peter, Ronnie and the crew. The ring I call my Elizabeth Taylor diamond, because I am sure that I treasure mine as much, if not more than she does, and it is probably as near as I shall ever get to a diamond.

We were still getting publicity about the film and in mid-January reporters and photographers from the Sun arrived wanting pictures of me (as mother) taking tea in a flask to Garrow (Tom). After ringing round various farms, we discovered that Garrow was over at Waldringfield ten miles away muck-spreading. Well it was no use trying to tell these town chaps where to go, so Ernie said he would take them, as it was down a very long lane. Before they set off they had all been sampling my home-made wines, Ernie too. Well, when they got back they looked as white as sheets. Ernie had obviously given them a rough ride round the lanes, and one of the reporters said, "I don't think your husband should drive .. or was it the wine?" After that little episode I wondered how we would get on when the lot from the Daily Mirror arrived. I made sure there wasn't too much wine out, just in case there was any driving to be done! Ted and Molly came too that time, and Ted arrived with a bunch of primroses and violets, the first of the year, saying, "I have brought flowers for the leading lady".

There were many happy occasions during that summer. I opened my first fete, at Shalford in Essex, complete with a fanfare! We had more and more visitors to the garden, and I was getting requests too to show parties round the 'Akenfield' locations. I even took part in a sponsored walk for 'Celebrities' to help the Samaritans. But one of my greatest pleasures was attending the wedding of Garrow and Helen at Earl Stonham. They had met while we were making the film.

But life is not all sweetness and honey, and we all have to learn to take the rough with the smooth, and while all these activities had been going on, Ernie had been ill, You never know with illness how much is physical and how much is mental, often it's a combination of both. Now Ernie had been worrying a great deal about his work. He had always been an honest and loyal worker, honesty and straight dealings were his standards. He had been promoted and this meant that he had to fill in a great number of forms for the other men and himself. The worry and responsibility of all this weighed heavily on Ernie and his mind was troubled. He had been unwell and he had been receiving treatment. I thought that the distraction of the film and the trips to London might do him good, but I had been worrying about him all the time.

He had been doing so well, and we had been making plans for the garden, deciding which seeds and plants were to go where, when, in March, he had a relapse. I wondered if the excitement of the past few weeks had all been too much for him, but he told me later that it was the thought of returning to work and facing all his mates, wondering what they would say and how they would react knowing that he had had treatment in a mental hospital. I told him that people would understand as so many people these days have psychiatric help. With patience and a lot of love, Ernie pulled through and was able to go back to work in April.

In June we featured in TV Times in an article called 'Stars and their Gardens'. I was beginning to feel like a 'Star' as I opened fetes, gave the prizes out at three schools and at flower shows as well as judging at others, but the hard work in our garden soon brought me back to reality.

Although my excursion into the film world was over (apart

from the television gardening programmes) I had not finished with the position I held during the filming of Akenfield as universal provider of odd objects. It was late autumn when Rex rang, about six in the evening, to ask if I could get him a sheep! A live one, not a carcass. He would be down to pick it up at ten. It was wanted, he added, by a musician friend of his, for a film he was making. Well, I've been asked to find some strange things since I got mixed up with these film people, but a fat lamb at that time of the year, and in four hours, was going to take some doing. After a number of telephone calls I located a shepherd, some twelve miles away, who agreed to sell me one on condition it was collected from him. I explained the position and told him it would probably be about 10.30 before they would be there.

Then began the wait. It was 11.30 before they arrived, and then there was a great long van pulled up outside, and Rex apologising for being late by saying they had collided with a Rolls-Royce outside Colchester. He took me out to meet his friends. They invited me into their home - that van was done out just like a travelling palace. One of them was making a meal on a portable stove. There it was, almost midnight, and we still hadn't picked up that blessed sheep, and these chaps seemed in no hurry - have some coffee they said. I began to wonder if the shepherd would still be up, so I chivvied them along, but it took ten minutes to back that van down our lane it was so long, and then we set off, me leading the way at twenty miles an hour. We eventually took possession of the sheep and I asked Rex where they were going to put it. "Oh," said one of the musicians, "in our home," and with that they lifted the blessed sheep onto a bunk bed all covered over with lovely rugs. The shepherd looked at me, "My God, I have seen it all now," he said.

AFTER AKENFIELD

Well, it is now 1995, and I have recently undergone an operation for breast cancer, and am currently receiving radium treatment, which, with God's blessing will allow me to continue my busy and fulfilling life, having suffered this sudden, definitely unwanted, and devasting intrusion within my life. As you can imagine, it is not good news for someone like me to be told to 'take things easy', as there is always something to do in the garden. I am finding however, that my writing and the garden, combined with the love and support of family and friends, are creating within me the 'willpower' to "beat this thing". My brief stay in hospital did however allow me time to reflect upon the passing years since 'Akenfield', and to recall the many pleasurable highlights which have occurred. I thought you might like to hear about a few of them, and hope you enjoy reading about them, as I have certainly enjoyed being a part of them.

There is no doubt that our lives did change somewhat after the filming of 'Akenfield' and those first years of having the garden open. It seemed strange to Ernie and me, that after all the years of getting different gardens into shape and doing something that we took for granted as being part of the natural course of things in the country, that is using the land you have got, to work for you to provide as much of your daily food as possible, that other people should be so interested in what we were doing.

And who would have thought years ago, that a country girl from Suffolk would have been invited to a 'Woman of The Year' luncheon at the Savoy Hotel in London? Well, in 1975 that is just what happened. I spent weeks looking for a coat, dress and hat for this special occasion. I ended up with a matching coat and dress in almond green silk, with a matching pill box hat with ostrich feathers at the back. And, yes, you've guessed it, that hat cost nearly as much as the coat and dress

*H R H the Princess Margaret and Lady Penn
are shown round the garden by Peggy Cole
during the private visit of Her Royal Highness*

Fresh berries straight from the cane really are irresistible!

together! My shoes, gloves and bag were brown. And so there I was, all dressed up to the nines, sitting down to luncheon with Mrs. Harold Wilson, Judith Chalmers, Shirley Williams and Lady Khama, wife of the ruler of Botswana. All those important and well known people - and me! It was a lovely episode, but to me it was no better than the thrill I got that same month when I decorated the church in the pretty village of Easton, with flowers for the wedding of my younger brother, Peter. For you see, flowers don't change, there's no class or social distinction for them. If you are involved with them, they don't mind who you are, neither will they change their ways and needs no matter how important or not that you are.

We had barely got used to the idea of folk coming to see our garden, first in small numbers, and then by the coach load, when next it was the national magazines and then TV companies wanting to write about us or make films about the garden and my wine making and so on. We had all sorts of interesting and important people come to see us and the garden, but it is not everyday that a Royal Princess comes to call!

One Tuesday, it was 31st July 1984, Lady Penn called to see me. As we walked around the garden she remarked that someone rather special wished to meet me, H.R.H. the Princess Margaret, I was speechless! Me? Just an ordinary country girl? When I asked Lady Penn why we were to be so honoured, she told me that Her Royal Highness had seen the film 'Akenfield' and had liked it so much that she had said she would like to meet me.

Can you imagine how I felt? I was almost numb for a few minutes, and then the thought went through my head over and over, 'a Princess coming to see me and walk round my garden! I had to come back to reality as Lady Penn talked about the practical arrangements to be made for the visit which was to take place, not at some vague date in the future, but on the very Friday of the same week, just three days to get myself ready! Lady Penn thought it would be best if we did not say anything about the visit beforehand so that H.R.H. would have the chance to make a really private visit.

155

I did ask if I could have my family present to meet her, particularly my brother Ron who does so much work in the garden these days. My request was granted, but how I got through those next three days, I shall never know, as I was bursting to tell my friends. Even my sons thought I was joking when I first told them.

At last the great day arrived, Friday 3rd August 1984. I was so nervous but I had no need to be, for the Princess is such a lovely lady that once the introductions were over, she made me feel at ease. Sir Eric and Lady Penn and two security officers came too, so it was just like having our very own small garden party. Princess Margaret is very knowledgeable about garden plants as I soon discovered as we walked around the garden. I told her all about opening for charity and I also showed her the wine shed and all the dried flowers I have hanging up in there.

Then it was into my sitting room to sit down and chat about village life, and how we made the film of 'Akenfield'. I was able to show her the stills of the film. I also told her about this book which I had just had accepted for publication. I also asked Her Royal Highness if she would mind me telling the W.I. and other clubs I attend about her visit, and she told me to tell the W.I. that we need young members. She is, of course, a member of the Womens Institute herself. I then presented her with a cheque for £100 for the N.S.P.C.C. of which she is the President (this was part of the proceeds from the garden) and she graciously accepted one of my dried flower arrangements, she then signed my 'Visitors' Book' and the visit was over. An hour had passed in a flash.

In 1980 I had been approached by the local Radio Station, at that time known as 'Radio Orwell', well, little did I think that the day would come when I would be introduced as a Radio Personality but it did. For several years I would travel twice weekly to Ipswich to participate in programmes on gardening and village life, with cookery recipes and old country remedies. This also led to 'Phone Ins' and I had much enjoyment in trying to answer questions and chatting to other local people who had similar interests to myself. This really did 'open up a can of worms' as I would receive telephone calls at home, from people asking me all sorts of things, and the postman was kept really busy, you should see some of the things that have dropped onto my doormat, from old photographs to pieces taken from plants and weeds. It has become quite a job keeping up with all the correspondence, but has provided me with much pleasure.

Since September 1987 I have been writing a weekly column on Country topics for the local newspaper company, 'The East Anglian Daily Times' based in Ipswich, this paper has a wide circulation, reaching all over East Anglia. This work I thoroughly enjoy, it has once again brought me many new friends and contacts, and has contributed to my heavy mail delivery, which in turn keeps me up to the mark on research into Country Lore etc.

In October 1987, I was invited by Mrs Patsy Hovenden, an American lady who had previously visited my garden, to lecture in the U.S.A. What an experience to be given the chance of, one not to be missed, although quite daunting as I had neither flown or been abroad before! However, as usual, after much encouragement from family and friends, I made up my mind to go. During the visit, I gave fourteen talks and travelled 10,000 miles in just twenty days, I sure was kept busy! This trip is featured in greater detail in my book 'Diary of A Country Woman'. It was whilst I was away on this trip, that the notorious October '87 Hurricane struck, and caused so much devastation to property and woodlands in the South and East of England; flattening almost the entire areas of Rendlesham and Tunstall Forests' in East Suffolk. What sights to come back to!

Leading seed people, Thompson and Morgan, in 1989 asked me if I would consider giving talks and demonstrations in 'Harrods' that famous Knightsbridge store. This was to be part of their promotional event on dried flowers. It entailed travelling to London one day a week for four weeks, by train and then underground, and yes, you're right, in the rush hour, how do people do it every day? I certainly longed to be back in my peaceful and serene Suffolk Village! Never-the-less it was a marvellous experience, there was much interest shown by the shoppers, in my talks, seed sowing and dried flower arranging demonstrations.

Then one day in 1991, I received a very unexpected and surprising invitation in the post, it was from Buckingham Palace, and was asking me to attend one the the Queen's Summer Garden Parties! What an honour. After the initial shock had gone, I was left with the daunting problem of what to wear? Being rather a large lady, I find comfort more than fashion to be the answer, and if I am really honest I have no interest what-so-ever in fashion, and I actually detest 'dressing up'. This problem had to be overcome, and luckily for me my local Co-op came to the rescue, kitting me out splendidly for the occasion.

I was not allowed to take an escort, but Allan and his family drove me to London, and as we were allowed to park in The Mall, they left me at the Palace, and went off to have a picnic in nearby St. James' Park. And little Sarah, was quite worried about me having to go to the 'tea party' on my own, and said, that if she had a hat, that perhaps they would let her in!

There I was standing in line with all the other guests, and what a line, there are between 6,000 and 8,000 invited to these occasions. Gradually we moved through the gates, then proceeded to walk straight through the palace and out into the grounds behind. It was the hottest day of the year, and I found myself feeling sorry for the poor men, who of course had to wear collar and tie. Finally The Queen appeared in an outfit of yellow, my first impression, was how small she looked, compared with seeing her on the telly. By this time we had formed lines, and she walked up and down, occasionally stopping to speak to people selected by the Ushers. Also present was the Duke of Edinburgh, Prince Charles and Lady Diana. When the formalities were over, the Queen took her place in the seats alongside the small marquee for the Royal Party.

Then it was time to mingle, quite daunting on my own as you

158

can imagine, but suddenly I caught sight of one friendly face, and that of someone I knew, it was our local Bishop John Dennis, who soon took me under his wing, and I was then lucky enough to be able to walk around with him and his wife. Phew!

The marquee was serving iced drinks, ice cream, and of course other light tea fare of sandwiches and cakes, but my goodness! did that heat from the sun have fun with the chocolate cake, it ran everywhere, not many takers for that.

After an extremely pleasant afternoon, of chatting to, and meeting various famous, and some not so famous but just as interesting people, it was time to leave, and to find Allan and family and set off for home, how I longed to get home and have a 'cup of tea'. Little did I know then, that I would one day return to the Palace for an even more exciting and honourable occasion.

Late in 1992, I received another 'out of the blue' proposition - this time an invitation issued by the Programme Controller for Entertainments on the QE2. This was to fly out to New York and sail back on the world's most famous liner, giving lectures as part of the shipboard entertainment en-route.

This was a wonderful weeks trip for me in several ways; first I went to Boston, where I had given a talk on my previous visit to the States in 1987. Then there were more lectures in New Jersey. Only two talks were required of me on the return trip to Southampton, so I had plenty of time to relax and enjoy the very luxurious surroundings on the Q.E.2., being waited on at every turn - and with never a thought from beginning to end about peeling potatoes or washing-up! The food, need I add, was out-of-this-world. Once again I found myself taking part in something that I probably would not even have dreamed about. I have to say that I felt quite guilty when I arrived home, having indulged in so much rich fare, so I settled down and made a simple country stew, to quickly bring me back to reality.

The next milestone in my life, once again was to have a 'Right Royal' flavour, in June of last year, 1993, I received notification that I had been named in the Queen's Honours list for an M.B.E. I quickly rang Allan to let him know, as I couldn't really believe it, he was so pleased for me, but he had some very sound advice for me, suggesting that I kept this to myself for the time being.

Later that month, on the day the official list is released to the press, I had a telephone call from the East Anglian Daily Times, they asked me if I had been keeping secrets from them, because of course they all knew me quite well by now. This was my confirmation that I really was to receive the M.B.E. later that year. The next day the list appeared in all the newspapers, I have to say that it took me quite some time to achieve getting up and dressed, let alone having a cup of tea, as the 'phone did not stop ringing, from family and friends wanting to congratulate me. Within two weeks of the announcement, I received a lovely cake when I visited the W.I. market, made specially for me. Then a little while later, Charsfield and Hoo P.C.C. put on a luncheon party for myself, family and friends, this was held at Hoo House, and after lunch another wonderful cake appeared, and I was also presented with a lovely china plate, inscribed with my name and the year to commemorate the M.B.E. award. What a generous and thoughtful gesture, and a wonderful keepsake for me.

Well, once again I was faced with the prospect of 'What to wear?', I was lucky enough to find my choice of outfit in Debenhams, it was a green and navy plaid suit, rather smart, though I say so myself, and I chose navy accessories.

This visit to the Palace, I was allowed to take my brother Ronnie, and both Allan and David, this was the first time since 1950 that Ronnie had been to London, he couldn't get over the amount of traffic, and how busy the streets were.

By now, of course, it was November, a traditionally icy cold day, and I have to say, that in all I have done over the years, the thousand of talks I have given and the people I have had to meet, that this was by far the most nerve-racking experience of my life. Luckily we arrived on schedule despite the icy conditions, and were shown into the reception area, where we were told what was to happen and of course, how we should act in front of Her Majesty. This is where I was to leave my family.

Finally it was my turn. The Queen asked my why I was being honoured in this way, and I replied that it was for charitable works as a result of the garden and film, I wanted to add that her sister had visited my garden, but before I knew it, the medal had been pinned on my lapel, and the Queen was shaking my hand, this was my cue to exit the room, and I had to leave backwards, as of course you must not turn your back on Her Majesty, my one fear was that I would trip over and make a fool of myself. Thank goodness I didn't.

After this was the photograph session, this took longer than the actual ceremony, and I have to add that we took a few of our own. And then we set off for home.

Since my original attendance at the 'Woman of the Year' Luncheon, I have been lucky enough to return twice more, in 1977 and 1989. On the last visit, that wonderful actress Patricia Routledge was the guest speaker, and during the event I was able to have a few minutes with H.R.H. Princess Margaret, and was able to hand over a donation in aid of the London Blind Association.

My greatest honour to date, has to be, of course, the award of the M.B.E., one that I shall treasure for the rest of my life, and a memory for my family to reflect upon when I am gone. I have to say that throughout all the years of hard work preceding this public recognition, that I have experienced constant pleasure from my modest plot of country land, and my hope is, that the happiness and contentment it has brought me, will, in some way, have rubbed-off on many of the thousands of appreciative visitors who have been to 'Akenfield' and who have perhaps stumbled across one of the many plaques to be found in the garden, such as the one which reads:-

The Kiss of the Sun for Pardon,
The Song of the Birds for Mirth.
One is Nearer to God's Heart in a Garden,
Than Anywhere else on Earth!

THE WOMEN'S INSTITUTE

The Princess was right about us needing more young members in the W.I. At one time the group in Charsfield had lapsed for a number of years, but I am pleased to say that I managed to get it going again because I feel that it has a valuable part to play in village life. Not only that, it gives every country woman who is a member the chance to voice her ideas and opinions about issues which affect her, her family and the community, as well as those larger problems of the nation as a whole. At the local level one of the highlights of the week for many of us is the W.I. Market. I for one, look forward to this very much as it is a good place to meet your friends and it offers you the chance of making a little pin-money by selling your produce.

The W.I. Markets are registered as Friendly Societies and are run on business-like lines. The Markets have a Chairman, a Treasurer and a Secretary elected from among the producers. A producer can become a shareholder in a W.I. Market for a membership of 5p. and you do not have to be a member of the W.I. so anyone, including male producers, is welcome to membership. A controller is appointed to price the goods and to look after the organisation and standards of the market. A small commission is deducted for overhead expenses, otherwise all the money taken for your produce is paid to you.

However, the produce sold is subject to the normal statutory regulations concerning weights and measures, labelling and hygiene. In our Market no shoddy goods are accepted, and good packaging and presentation are among the main aims. All the jams, pickles and so on have to have labels which show the main ingredients and the weight and also the name of the producer. Actually, every item of produce has to carry the name of the producer, so if there is any come-back, the person concerned can be located.

For those of you who have never been to a W.I. Market, here is a sample of what you could expect to see on sale. Bread, the really good home-baked varieties, cakes of all shapes and sizes, pies, savouries etc. - and if you were giving a special party, you could order items for it in advance and know that it would all be as near perfect as can be. Then there are all the items of garden produce, flowers, fruit, vegetables, plants, eggs, honey, jams, jellies, chutneys and pickles. And then there are the crafts; some of the items at the Markets are better than any of your Bond Street goods. The work in them is excellent and the items are made to last. The W.I. is of course famous for its knitting and various branches of needlework, but you will also find woodwork, metalwork and other crafts, often produced not by specialist craftsmen, but by ordinary country girls like me.

The Women's Institute has over the years, given me a great deal, and I hope I have been able to repay some of the debt I owe, by going round to different groups to talk. They are always most interested in the one I call "The Making of Akenfield" and I must have given this nearly four thousand times now. Also I write an article on gardening for the W.I. monthly newspaper, so this is another way in which I am able to contribute to this wonderful institution.

CURRENT AND
FAMILY AFFAIRS

I think the fact that I'm proud to be a Suffolk Mawther (girl) and that I've got a pretty strong dialect and a rather round about way of saying things, makes people like my talks, because you know, I don't think facts by themselves are very interesting. Life doesn't work in straight and separate lines, growing a garden reminds you of that all the time, and life and talking are interesting, because of the decorations and frills you give them, or in other words, the colour, like a garden. And talking of the way we speak, they even made a programme about the way Ernie and I talked which went out on the B.B.C. World Service.

Our lives, as you have heard, changed when the garden and film brought us into the limelight, and my life has changed again with the sad loss of Ernie. It is now 14 years since he passed away, suddenly in his sleep, and I have had to come to terms with the fact that life must go on for the rest of us. There have been times when it is hard to carry on, when behind the smile there has been sadness and worry, but with God's help I have come through. I have realised how important it is to be able to meet people and have activities to carry on with when you have lost your partner. I am still young enough to get out and about, and when I am feeling a little down, I can jump in my car and visit my family, but I also understand the senior citizen who having lost their partner, find themselves unable to do anything but gaze at an 'empty chair'.

Helping me along the way, came the arrival of the greatest gift any child can give to a parent, given to me by Allan and his wife Jackie, the next generation, Russell Ernest, my first grandchild. When Allan 'phoned to tell me the news, it was as if part of my beloved Ernie was back in this world. Russell who is now ten years, has been joined by his sister Sarah Jenny, (now nine years). And David and his wife Norine have added to our merry band with George Ernest, who is just two

165

My grandchildren

Sarah Jenny   *George*   *Russell*

years, and we have recently heard that he is to have a baby brother or sister later this year. I feel very lucky knowing that the family name will continue in years to come. And of course, like any proud Grandma, I thoroughly enjoy having the grandchildren to stay at weekends and during some of the school holidays.

Since losing Ernie, I have bought my council house and with the untiring help of my dear brother Ronnie, have maintained and developed the garden to the evident delight of our summer visitors. It was always 'Ernies Dream' to "own our own home" and now I hope, please God, that I can stay here until I am carried out 'in a box' for my last journey in this life.

Home improvements which I have been able to organise over recent years have included, central heating (a Parkray fire with radiators) a new bathroom and shower, a small conservatory on the back of the house and re-felting of the roof. So I have all the comforts I need, although I still often wish I had a nice big kitchen and a large pantry, especially when I'm up to the elbows in a big baking session for a special village event! But one cannot hope to have every wish granted, and my tried and tested methods get me through.

Over the years I participated in 'pool' nursing. This meant I was on call to help out at the hospital when short staffed. As mentioned before, I also had a part-time job at St. Audry's Psychiatric Hospital in Melton, this I left in 1984. This was with some regret as I had enjoyed the work, but it was both physically and mentally exhausting on top of all my other commitments, such as Council and Church work, show judging and broadcasting on the local radio. Then in 1993, as a result of quite severe cut-backs by the Government in N.H.S. funding, St.Audry's was closed down, this made me very sad indeed.

In 1991 I ended my broadcasting days at Radio Orwell, when the station was taken over by another company and turned into an all-music channel. During the ten years in which I was running my weekly 'Peggy's Patch' on the station, I made many friends, especially among other gardeners in the region. I have missed this form of social contact. I am however still occasionally asked by other radio stations in the region to do talks on various aspects of country life.

Television crews from the B.B.C., I.T.V. and Channel Four have over the years continued to visit and film the garden, with leading gardening presenters such as, Geoff Hamilton, Peter Seabrook and Geoffrey Smith. Anna Pavord had two programmes in her 1991 Channel 4 series 'Flowering passions' and for once Ronnie was featured as well as myself, he was seen working away at the watering. That warm-hearted actress Thora Hird did one of her summer programmes from here for her series 'Praise Be' on B.B.C. I in 1993, and Patrick Anthony came and actually baked an exotic cake in my tiny kitchen for his 'Good Food Guide' programme on I.T.V. in July of the same year.

I have also received the honour of having a Fuchsia named after me, and also there is one named 'Akenfield' in joint tribute to Ronald Blythe's wonderful book and film and the garden.

Over the years two more books have been added to this first title, they are, 'Country Cottage Companion' published by David and Charles in 1988, and 'Diary of a Country Woman' published by Morrow and Co. in 1991, both books cover the subject dearest to my heart - gardening, country wisdom, and country cooking.

My 'Akenfield' garden continues to flourish, and each year it seems to open doors to various functions, events and new experiences, it is included in the 'Annual Survey of Gardens in England and Wales' produced by the National Gardens, and also in the 'Good Gardens Guide to Britain and Ireland'. These books are to let people know which gardens are open to the public, and list and describe the note-worthy ones, so this is quite an honour. Mine is, I think, still the only 'Council House Garden' listed, although it is now of course privately owned. And even though it is so widely known now, it still continues to be a simple cottage garden, in a still unspoilt corner of rural Suffolk.

The 'gate money' from the garden has always and continues to be donated to local charities, and to date more than £53,000 has been handed over to many causes. I gain much pleasure from being able to do this from simply carrying out my hobby of gardening which gives me such enjoyment anyway. Every now and then, I receive some sort of recognition for this charity work, and although I have never asked or wanted any reward, it is pleasing to know that people appreciate the gifts received. The largest share of the charity money goes to the very worthy cause of The Saint Elizabeth Hospice in Ipswich, who do such wonderful work, and they have honoured me by making me a Patron. The Ipswich Rotary Club presented me with a framed certificate for 'Services to the Community'. It seems strange to me to receive such honours for simply doing something you love.

In a world that is constantly faced with changes to life styles, due to technology, the increase of crime, the high rate of drug abuse and of course disease and illness, I find much comfort in my own life style in this small village, which to some may seem outdated. In spite of this I keep myself up to date and aware of the changes happening around me. Coping with change is not a new experience for country folk, it is simply the pace of change which is so different from anything we have known before. Perhaps the 'computer' is the most obvious example of this, now reaching from every corner of 'Big Business' to, yes, even the farm! Technology recently came to Charsfield when Farming Press Videos of Wharfedale Road, Ipswich, made a video called "An English Cottage Garden". In this film Ronnie and I give an insight into our garden and the traditional country life.

There is of course the recent recession, which has brought upon us the sort of poverty not seen in our 'fair land' since the early nineteen-thirties. When we however reflect on the conflict in Bosnia and other parts of the world, we must surely feel that we still have much to be thankful for.

I have been blessed with an active mind, and this led to me holding the position of Village Recorder, which has meant

169

keeping an eye on the changes within the village, taking photographs of all the houses, and taking them again as any alterations are made. This is to provide an accurate record of what life has been like for future reference. I have found this work to be very interesting and stimulating.

Also as a member of the Parish Council, I have been lucky enough to help influence the way things go for my beloved Charsfield. Unfortunately the fight given by the council was not enough to prevent the closure and great loss of the last remaining shop in the village, and even worse the Post Office.

On an even sadder note, having previously mentioned in an earlier revision note for this book, several old friends and local characters have passed on from our community and indeed this life. Another sad loss locally, was the tragic death in a boating accident on the river Deben in 1993, of the brilliant Suffolk artist, John Western. John, who lived and worked in nearby Monewden, created many splendid water-colour paintings and line drawings of Suffolk Scenes. His original works are greatly sought after, whilst his calendar reproductions have in the past been an annual delight to his less well off admirers.

Within my own family there have been changes too, my sons Allan and David as you know are now grown up and have left home, both now have families of their own, perhaps more importantly they both made the choice to 'leave the land', in doing so, breaking a tradition of generations, but none-the-less I am very proud of them both, for they represent the future, they are educated, and have both qualified as police officers. They have before them the opportunity to achieve the highest positions within their chosen profession.

Earlier, I mentioned that when Russell Ernest was born, that I felt a small part of my beloved Ernie had returned, well, I believe that everything comes back, only in a different way, and that whatever the time, there is a bit of you living somewhere. That's why I'm a country girl at heart, because I see reflections of myself and my family, and everything I love and hold dear to me in all that is around me.

Who would have guessed that my life could have been filled with such wonderful experiences as you have now heard about. What a lucky person I am. To think, that all this has happened to me, *'JUST AN ORDINARY COUNTRY GIRL'*.

Index to Recipes